# When Disability Hits Home

# When Disability Hits Home

## How God Magnifies His Grace in Our Weakness and Suffering

Paul Tautges

with contributions from

Joni Eareckson Tada

*Shepherd Press*
*Wapwallopen, Pennsylvania*

When Disability Hits Home

All body text © 2020 Paul Tautges

All text under the headings *From Joni's Heart. . .*
© 2020 Joni Eareckson Tada

ISBN
Paper:  978-1-63342-192-9
epub:  978-1-63342-193-6
Kindle:  978-1-63342-194-3

NOTE: A Scripture Index is included in the paper version only.

**Shepherd Press**
P.O. Box 24
Wapwallopen, PA 18660

www.shepherdpress.com

Typography by **documen**

# Contents

# Endorsements

With compassion and insider insight, Paul Tautges shows from Scripture how God's providence, purposes, and goodness address the very real struggles and honest questions of those suffering physical and intellectual disability. The chapter-ending touches from Joni bring further wisdom and comfort. My counseling students will certainly know about this book.

**Robert D. Jones**, DMin, Southern Baptist Theological Seminary, author of *Pursuing Peace* and *Uprooting Anger*

Paul Tautges and Joni Eareckson Tada pack into this small volume a boatload of profound truths that every believer needs to hear and live: "God makes no distinction between quality of life and life itself." "God, not disability, is front and center." "A person's identity is not defined by his or her disabilities." "Some of God's best gifts must be unwrapped in the dark." Never have I seen so much biblical truth about how to suffer well to the glory of God put into such a compassionate, powerful, and Word-filled discussion! My own church, Faith Baptist Church in Taylors, SC, is the home for Hidden Treasure Christian School, a ministry of Christian education to several dozen special needs children and teens. This book, I'm sure, will become a key tool for both parents and staff in carrying out that mission more effectively in the days ahead. But beyond that, we are all broken. We all need to learn to suffer well to the glory of our Savior!

**Jim Berg**, DMin, Professor of Biblical Counseling, Bob Jones University Seminary; Executive Director, Freedom That Lasts; and author of *Changed into His Image* and *Quieting a Noisy Soul*

# Foreword

In 1995 I would have hated this book. My eldest son was born without eyes, and, as a result, I rejected God and thought he was sadistically cruel. I ended all association with my church, small group, and Christian friends. The biblically based, God-centered focus of this book would have felt barbaric and ridiculous at that time.

Today, however, I love what Paul Tautges and Joni Eareckson Tada have created. What can explain my change? The answer is that God used two ordinary people who saw my son as a human being made in the image of his God rather than as a pitiful, broken project. This couple believed everything articulated in this book about God, his character, and his good purposes. They didn't know much about disability, but they knew how to live and love with confidence that God would provide for them and for me.

You probably found or were given this book because you are directly impacted in some way by disability. If so, I pray that the truths from God's Word and the wisdom applied by Paul and Joni will penetrate into the deepest places of your heart for your comfort and, yes, even a rising joy in Jesus Christ.

But this book is not only for you. In fact, it may not be primarily for families like yours and mine who are experiencing disability. Here's what I mean.

If you want to energize a room of people impacted by disability, whether in themselves or in a family member, ask them to talk about their experiences at church. Energy and passion will rise quickly, frequently including tears. Many of us have hard stories to share about foolish and callous things people have said to us at church, sometimes even asserting that their perspectives came from God's Word. And too many families like ours have even been encouraged to find another place to worship, told that they are no longer welcome *at church* because of disability in one or more of their family members.

Thankfully, this book provides an answer. Paul, as both a pastor and a father, carefully considers and applies God's Word and provides insight into how that Word impacts a father's heart. Joni, who for decades has encouraged people all over the world to embrace God as sovereign and good in the midst of the hardest things, provides her usual wisdom and insight that will model for leaders how to help their people who are facing difficult issues.

From that perspective, this book is especially for pastors, elders, and leaders of every kind in our churches. When pastors and teachers study, pray, wrestle with, and then lead their people into God's Word on disability, the church can become a refuge of peace and comfort for families in a culture that hates disability and people with disabilities. And the church benefits when the gifts of people with disabilities, gifts granted by God himself (Ephesians 2:10), are used in our churches.

As I write this, my now twenty-five-year-old son is swinging in his hammock, singing a song only he understands, and enjoying a pleasant summer morning. He is blind, severely cognitively impaired, epileptic, and on the severe end of Autism Spectrum Disorder. Through a quarter century of chaos every promise from God's Word found in this book has proven true. May you read and cling to each promise, expectant that God will also meet you in your deepest pain, providing peace and joy found only in Jesus Christ.

**John Knight**, Desiring God Ministries

# Introduction

The idea for this book was conceived in April 2011 at The Gospel Coalition conference in Chicago, during two conversations that could only have been providentially arranged by God. The first was with a representative from a small publisher I had admired from a distance for a long time. The second was with a total stranger who, in a matter of hours, became a dear friend.

My conversation with Rick, the publisher's acquisitions editor, began simply as two dads talking about our families, catching up with each other since the last time we had seen each other at a conference. Since he knew that some of our children had been born with hearing impairment, Rick asked if I'd ever thought about writing on the topic of disability and parenting. I hadn't, but I was open to thinking about it. However, when I shared with him my passion for thinking through all forms of suffering from a theological perspective, he enthusiastically introduced me to someone else. "Come with me," he said.

Rick brought me down the hall to the Desiring God Ministries display area. There I met a man named John Knight. "You two need to talk," Rick said.

What commenced was a couple hours of kindred conversation, two dads bonding instantly, sharing our hearts with one another over matters related to God, disability, and the church. He then asked, "Have you ever thought about preaching a sermon series and writing a book about disability? I think it's God's will for you."

*Well, that was certainly bold!*

We ended our visit by tearfully praying for one another and

the church worldwide to awaken to the need to think biblically about disability and the suffering it brings. Then I found a quiet spot, sat down in a comfortable chair, and began writing in my journal. I was not, however, prepared for my emotional reaction. Here's what I wrote:

> *April 13, 2011, 2:30 PM*
>
> *Sitting in a soft, cozy chair at The Gospel Coalition conference in Chicago, I just wiped away tears that have been streaming down my face. For two hours we talked, cried, shared our lives and prayed with each other.*
> *Thank you, Lord, for bringing John Knight of Desiring God Ministries into my life. This divine appointment was such a display of your kindness to me!*
> *Why am I crying? I've not cried like this . . . over this [disabilities in our family] since Kayte was born [and she's now six]. Yes, I've cried with you, my God. Yes, I've cried with Karen, my precious wife. But I've not cried with another father—a father of a child with disabilities. John's son is not only blind, but he was born without eyes. My four hearing-impaired children at least have ears, and they are not at all disfigured. And three of them now have digital "ears" (cochlear implants). Here is a man who understands! Here is a 2 Corinthians 1:4 comforter! Yes, others have cared. Others have prayed. But not at this level. Not with a level of compassion that can only be birthed by suffering. O Lord, if this book idea ever comes to fruition, may it be that it will serve others as the Spirit served me, through John, today.*

When I returned to the church that I pastored in Wisconsin, I knew that my next sermon series had to be called "Disability and the Glory of God." The congregation welcomed and received the messages well, since the studies helped everyone to think more biblically about their own level of suffering, especially those whose families were in some way affected by disability. Those initial messages became the ground for multiple saplings to be planted, which have been growing for the past nine years.

The book you now hold in your hand is the fruit of the encouragement that I received from a handful of faithful friends. Rick wouldn't let me leave the conference without my agreeing to send him a book proposal. And John has never let me forget his heartfelt conviction that it was God's will for me, first, to preach a sermon series on disability and, second, to write this book. Little did I know that, years later, the Lord would begin to nurture a relationship between me and the ministry of the Joni & Friends International Disability Center. Without the reassuring words of numerous brothers and sisters in Christ, and kind encouragement from Joni Eareckson Tada, who enthusiastically agreed to contribute a personal reflection to close each chapter, this book would never have been written.

Compared to the suffering of many others, my wife and I consider our family's experience to be minor. Nonetheless, we are familiar with disability. Four of our ten children are affected by congenital hearing impairment, one of whom also has cognitive disabilities and autism. This ongoing experience, alongside almost three decades of pastoral ministry, has given me the opportunity to think about this topic from the viewpoint of Scripture. It's helped me to embrace and articulate a theology of suffering that is strong enough to stand up to the challenges of disability. My prayer is that the rock-solid truths of Scripture explained in this book will bring comfort and stability to your heart and mind, and also enrich your faith.

May 2020
Mayfield Heights, Ohio

# Chapter 1

# Whose Fault Is It?

*For from him and through him and to him are all*
*things. To him be glory forever. Amen.*

(Romans 11:36)

Fifteen years ago, my wife and I were standing in the kitchen of the old farmhouse we had planned to renovate. She said, with tears streaming down her face, "What did I do wrong? Was it something I ate during my pregnancy? Or was it something I failed to eat? Is God punishing our daughter for something I've done? Am I the cause of our precious little Kayte being born deaf?" As I held my wife, her heart did not agonize alone. I was also asking questions, though only inwardly: "Lord, I've given my whole life to your service, and been willing to sacrifice everything earthly. Is that not good enough? What more must I do to earn your favor? Is it my fault our daughter is cognitively disabled? Are you angry at me?"

Let me be clear. My wife and I would *never* choose a different life—that is, life without the blessings of disability. But as we've walked this journey together with the Lord for over three decades there have been times when, in our weakness, we've struggled with doubts like anyone else.

Perhaps you've asked similar questions. For you or your family it may not be deafness or autism, but some other physical or developmental disability. Perhaps it's Down syndrome, a life-debilitating accident or stroke, spina bifida, an unnamed disease, an untraceable learning disability, a growth hormone deficiency, or _____ (you fill in the blank). Whatever it is, it's now part of your life. I understand how you may feel.

When unanticipated suffering enters our personal world it's not unusual for our knee-jerk reaction to be one of wanting to identify the cause. We want to know *why*. When the mystery hits close to home the search for answers about disease, disorder, and disability can become more intense. The realization that your loved one or you yourself may have to live out your remaining days on earth with a malady for which there is no cure may lead to more provocative questions, like: Who is being punished by the Almighty? Is God really good? When disability hits home, our tendency as humans is to be driven by emotional reactions, rather than by truth. That is, we tend to let our emotions drive the car instead of our will governed by biblical truth. That's why we need a theological guide, or framework of thinking, that is built upon the Scriptures alone.

## A Trifold Framework for Thinking about the Works of God

In the most basic sense of the word, *theology* refers to how we think about God. In light of this, and because we all think about God in certain ways, every person is a theologian. The question remains, however, whether or not we are good theologians. Is how we think about God governed by how he has already revealed himself in Scripture, or have we invented our own theology? Have we created God in our own image instead of seeking to better understand what it means to be created in his image and for the purpose of bringing him glory?

To begin to answer questions like these it's essential to understand that sound theology begins and ends with doxology. That is to say, everything that God does will bring him glory in the end, and when we entrust ourselves to his kind and gracious care, our hearts will respond in praise to him.

If theology does not begin with doxology—the supreme exaltation of God—it will end up diminishing God's glory by exalting man. This, in the end, robs God of the glory and praise that belong to him alone. Therefore, any attempt to formulate a theology of suffering that is sturdy enough to embrace disability must begin and end with God. Romans 11:36 sums up theology with this doxology: "For from him and through him and to him are all things. To him be glory forever. Amen." The first word, "For," signals a response to the glorious truths the apostle has taught thus far in his letter, and the doxology acknowledges his sovereignty over all:

○ All things are *from* God.

○ All things live *through* God.

○ And all things are *to* God—that is, to the praise of his glory.

We will return to this trifold framework shortly, but for now it suffices to say that these three statements form an interpretive grid through which we can filter all of life's experiences.

## Two Common Temptations

In our attempt to understand God's ways in the midst of our suffering there are two common temptations which often fight to claim the higher ground in our mind.

### The Temptation to Blame Someone

Automatically connecting *personal* suffering to *personal* sin is a typical human response. "Since God is good," we reason, "he cannot be behind this accident, tragedy, or evil. Therefore, it must be the fault of the one who suffers or someone connected to him or her." Thankfully, the Holy Spirit wrote the Old Testament book of Job at least in part to correct that response.

The book of Job is essential to our understanding of suffering because it destroys the credibility of the notion that all suffering is the result of the sin of the sufferer. Theologian D. A. Carson says it well when he explains Job's unique contribution to our theology:

> *the book's special contribution to the canon [of Scripture], and to the topic of evil and suffering, is its treatment of what most of us would call irrational evil,*

*incoherent suffering. Such evil and suffering do not easily fit into glib "solutions." We may remember lessons learned elsewhere in the Bible, but when we try to apply them here there are too many loose ends. The physical suffering, as bad as it is, is compounded in Job's mind because it does not make any sense. Consequently, it threatens to destroy his understanding of God and the world, and is therefore not only massively painful in its own right, but disorienting and confusing.*[1]

On top of this, the pain and disillusionment of suffering is multiplied exponentially when accusations arise not only from our own doubtful hearts, but from the mouths of others—sometimes our own family or friends.

This is illustrated in the suffering of Job, whose friends believed their role in his life was to play private investigator, judge, and prosecuting attorney all wrapped into one, and to interrogate him about the cause of his suffering. They could not fathom that Job was not at least somehow responsible for the death of his ten children, the loss of his real estate and family fortune, or the painful sores covering his body from head to toe. The urgency of these miserable counselors to judge their hurting friend stemmed from their incomplete theology of God. D. A. Carson explains, "Job's friends [had] a tight theology with no loose ends. Suffering [was] understood exclusively in terms of punishment or chastening. There [was] no category for innocent suffering: in their understanding, such a suggestion besmirches the integrity of the Almighty."[2]

When we fast-forward to the New Testament, we find the disciples had the same incomplete theology, which resulted in asking the wrong question. As they wrestled with the problem of congenital disability, the disciples struggled to figure out who should be held responsible for causing a man to be blind from birth (John 9:1–12). They asked, "Rabbi, who sinned, this man or his parents?" To which the Savior replied, "It was not that this man sinned, or his parents, but that the works of God might be displayed in him." Clearly, the governing force behind this man's disability was not any one person's sin, but God's larger agenda to display his work and the glory of his grace. (We look at this incident in more detail in Chapter 3.)

Let's be honest. It's common for us to struggle with theological "loose ends." Our mind craves a "tight" theology about God that we are able to understand completely. We want a theology that leaves little room for true faith, mystery, wonder, or unanswered questions. As a result, disability can present a second temptation, which is to remake God in our image and likeness.

## The Temptation to Remake God in Our Image

If our conception of God is that he is only, or predominantly, love, and by this we mean that he does *only* what *we* perceive as good (for example, whatever does not involve pain), then irrational suffering tempts us to change our view of God to match our experience.

An example of this is found in Nancy Eiesland's influential book *The Disabled God: Toward a Liberatory Theology of Disability.* The author, a college professor in Atlanta and a lifelong sufferer of congenital bone defect, argued for the freedom of persons with disabilities from their socially disadvantaged prison, which must be accomplished by making the church "a body of justice for people with disabilities."[3] In order to achieve this, however, she openly asserted that the traditional Christian understanding of the Bible must be changed. As a result, she rejected the scriptural view of God's sovereignty over all, mocked "righteous submission to divine testing," and referred to biblical support for virtuous suffering as "particularly dangerous theology for persons with disabilities."[4] In short, she demanded a theology that "locates us [the disabled] at the speaking center."[5] But herein lies the age-old problem of man: demanding to be at the center of all things, and thereby rejecting a God-centered worldview.

To locate the person with a disability at the center Eiesland could not accept the plain reading of the Bible, because the God revealed there did not seem to fit neatly with her experience. Therefore, she longed for an epiphany that would begin with the experience of people with disabilities, and she waited for a new "revelation of God." And she got it. She wrote, "I saw God in a sip-puff wheelchair, that is, the chair used mostly by quadriplegics enabling them to maneuver by blowing and sucking on a straw-like device. Not an omnipotent, self-sufficient God, but neither a pitiable, suffering servant. In this moment, I beheld God as a survivor, unpitying and forthright."[6]

This epiphany, she said, enabled her to "offer a vision of a God who is for us [the disabled]."[7] Eiesland was correct to argue that the heart of God most certainly is turned toward those who suffer, but, sadly, the vision of God she offers is one made in her own image. Hence the title of her book, *The Disabled God*. To remake God in her own disabled image, she admitted, required "changing the symbol of Christ from that of suffering servant, model of virtuous suffering, or conquering lord, toward a formulation of Jesus Christ as disabled God."[8] To accomplish this, she stripped the resurrection of Christ of its power over sin and death. Instead, she claimed the resurrection was God's admission that he, too, is disabled, and always will be. "In presenting his impaired body to his startled friends," she wrote, "the resurrected Jesus is revealed as the disabled God."[9] Therefore, "God remains a God whom the disabled can identify with . . . he is not cured and made whole; his injury is part of him."[10]

Later, when the *New York Times* announced Nancy Eiesland's death at the age of forty-four, it opened the article with these words:

> By the time the theologian and sociologist . . . was
> 13 years old, she had had 11 operations for the
> congenital bone defect in her hips and realized pain was
> her lot in life. So why did she say she hoped that when
> she went to heaven she would still be disabled?
>
> The reason . . . was that her identity and character
> were formed by the mental, physical, and societal
> challenges of her disability. She felt that without her
> disability, she would "be absolutely unknown to myself
> and perhaps to God."[11]

This sad conclusion reinforces the need for us all to understand disability from a biblical perspective and, as a beneficial fruit, to minister faithfully to one another. To understand our own experience with disability, and be faithful to others who suffer, we must maintain that (1) God, not disability, is front and center; and (2) a person's identity is not defined by his or her disabilities.

Irrational suffering can drive the human heart to either reject God's sovereignty over all, or bring it to the place of surrendered faith. To say it another way, our response to disability (or any other type of suffering, for that matter) either keeps God at the center—where he alone belongs—or elevates man to take his place. Therefore, a faithful response to suffering requires that we submit our minds to God's mind as revealed in Scripture. Biblical faith recognizes God's ways as higher than man's ways, his thoughts as higher than ours (Isaiah 55:8–9). In short, we are not permitted to customize our theology. It originates either from Scripture or from man's wisdom. Therefore, we must turn to the Word of God for trustworthy counsel.

> Your testimonies are my delight;
> they are my counselors.
>
> (Psalm 119:24)

> Trouble and anguish have found me out,
> but your commandments are my delight.
>
> (Psalm 119:143)

By following the psalmist's example, my goal is to lead you to delight in God's Word so that, in turn, you may worship and adore the God who is revealed there.

How do we understand our suffering in light of the glory of God? How does biblical hope, which is rooted in Christ, empower us to live with purpose and joy, even when life's challenges threaten to overtake us? How do we view the inclusion of those with disabilities into the family of the local church? These are the kinds of questions I aim to answer in this book.

The place to begin is at the foundation: God's absolute authority and unwavering care.

## The Foundation of God's Providence
(All things are *from* God)

God's sovereignty, his rule over all, is the bedrock certainty for a proper theology of suffering. However, his sovereignty alone is not enough: we must maintain its connection to his goodness and wisdom. If we do not maintain this connection, we lose our perspective of God as the one who intimately cares for his creation, and we thereby undermine hope. Theologians refer to this connection as *providence*, which is one of the most comforting doctrines in the Bible.

### What Is Providence?

By *providence* we mean God employs his sovereign power and wisdom to continuously preserve every part of his creation and guide it toward his intended purpose. Sometimes people misinterpret sovereignty as a cold, sterile, and lifeless doctrine, but it is nothing of the sort. In his gracious providence, God carries out his sovereign rule in loving wisdom and attentive care. God is the sovereign ruler of the universe, to be sure, but he is also kind and a tender Father toward those who place their faith and hope in the Lord Jesus Christ. This brings us great comfort when we are in the midst of suffering that appears to have no purpose or end in sight.

The doctrine of providence rounds out bold statements of absolute sovereignty, like that of Psalm 115:3, "Our God is in the heavens; he does all that he pleases." Providence refers to the outworking of the sovereign rule of God—together with his wisdom and love—on behalf of the good of his creation, and especially for those who are redeemed by the precious blood of Christ.

Providence therefore assures us that, in his sovereignty, God is at work carrying out his perfect decrees for our good and his glory. It assures us that God is not far away, but always near. He is attentive to all of our ways and needs.[12] With the psalmist we say to God, "You are good and do good; teach me your statutes" (Psalm 119:68). Or as Job testifies, "Does not [God] see my ways and number all my steps?" (Job 31:4).

## God Is the Primary Caregiver

God's sovereignty is the truth which assures us that, regardless of secondary causes of disability, God remains in the primary position. Secondary causes are endless: genetic abnormalities, disease, work-related accidents, birth defects, war and civil violence, athletic injuries, drunk drivers who run through red lights, failed suicide attempts, abuse . . . the list goes on. But the primary cause is singular: God. The good, wise, kind, sovereign Creator and Sustainer of all never ceases to watch over his creation for his glory and our good. For example,

○ *If disability results from individual choices,* we can rest in knowing that "The heart of man plans his way, but the LORD establishes his steps" (Proverbs 16:9).

○ *If disability results from the harmful actions of others,* we can rest in knowing that what man means for evil, God can certainly work for good (Genesis 50:20; Romans 8:28).

○ *If suffering has no reasonable explanation,* we can rest in knowing that God is good, wise, and kind—and he does all things according to his purpose (Ephesians 1:11).

The mercy and nearness of our sovereign God bring much comfort to us. He is our primary caregiver.

Trusting God's infinite wisdom to govern all things will enable our hearts to be planted firmly in the ground, even if our legs are shaking. Our joy can remain when our faith rests in knowing that God is using both every pleasant and every painful experience to complete his redemptive purposes. Disability provides a conscious opportunity for us, the clay, to turn to the Potter and say, "Thy will be done."

## Four Pillars of Truth
(All things live *through* God)

Resting on the stable foundation of God's providence are four essential truths which form a framework for thinking biblically about disability and which support the weight of God's glory. These truths will be more fully developed throughout this book.

### Pillar #1:
### Every Human Being Is Created in God's Image and for His Purpose and, Therefore, Is of Immeasurable Value

When the deafness of our seventh baby was confirmed (while she was still an infant), my thoughts quickly turned to the words spoken by God to Moses: "Who has made man's mouth? Who makes him mute, or deaf, or seeing, or blind? Is it not I, the LORD?" (Exodus 4:11). "If God takes credit for making some people deaf," I concluded, "then he must have very good reasons for it. Therefore, it is not my place to question his holy purpose; instead, I should glory in his infinite wisdom. If cognitive disability is part of what God knows is good for our family, and provides unique opportunities to glorify him, then the Holy Spirit will enable us to rejoice in Christ and give thanks."

This response was not stoic. Neither were we guilty of what some might call *denial*. Our emotions were real. When my wife and I realized that of the hundreds of times we had told our daughter we loved her, not once had she heard us, pain was felt deep inside that words fail to describe. But God knows how much we treasure each of our ten children, and Kayte knows she is treasured too, even though now, at sixteen years of age, autism leads her to be content with very little affection.

For decades, abortion rights and "death with dignity" advocates have used "quality of life" talk to advance their agenda, but God makes no distinction between quality of life and life itself. Every human life, whether typical or disabled, is valuable in the eyes of the Creator. One of the beauties of disability is that it challenges us to measure our value of human life by one thing, and one thing alone: the image-of-God stamp that it bears. The sanctity of human life—unborn, already born, disabled, or elderly—remains rooted in one concrete truth: that every human being is a divine image-bearer and, therefore, invaluable. Holding firmly to this pillar shifts our view from the outer person to the inner person who lives under the never-ending, intentional gaze of God, regardless of the condition of the body he or she may occupy for the time being.

Pillar #2:
Gospel Treasure Is Hidden in Earthen Vessels
But Made More Visible through Suffering

The Bible is transparent about the variety of afflictions that believers endure, both in body and in spirit. In one place, the apostle Paul describes his varied experience this way:

> But we have this treasure in jars of clay, to show
> that the surpassing power belongs to God and
> not to us. We are afflicted in every way, but not
> crushed; perplexed, but not driven to despair;
> persecuted, but not forsaken; struck down, but
> not destroyed; always carrying in the body the
> death of Jesus, so that the life of Jesus may also
> be manifested in our bodies. For we who live are
> always being given over to death for Jesus' sake, so
> that the life of Jesus also may be manifested in our
> mortal flesh.
>
> (2 Corinthians 4:7–11)

Christians are jars of clay; we are common vessels. In these weak frames we experience various afflictions of both body and spirit. But within our mortal frames dwells something else: the hope found only in Jesus Christ.

When we believe the gospel we are united to Christ, and his Spirit takes up residence within us and makes the life of Jesus more visible. In light of this confident hope, physical disability may be more than tolerated: it may be received as one means of training our hearts to cling to the promise of God's enduring presence. Cognitive and physical afflictions are opportunities to magnify the worth of Jesus our Lord, in order "to make us rely not on ourselves but on God who raises the dead" (2 Corinthians 1:9).

## Pillar #3:
## Weakness Is a Platform for God's Sufficient Grace and Power to Be Displayed in Loving Community

God's greater purpose for disability includes the expansion of a platform for the display of his unsurpassed grace, power, and love within the normal functioning of Christian community. Though the Spirit intentionally hid from us the identification of Paul's most nagging affliction, we do know his "thorn in the flesh" was ultimately given to him by God, custom designed and delivered through Satan, for the purpose of teaching the apostle humility (2 Corinthians 12:1–10). Without this affliction, the apostle would have been less useful to God. Paul's chronic affliction was so painful that he believed he could no longer live *with* it, so he pleaded with God to take it away. But the Lord knew differently; he knew that the apostle could not properly live for God *without* it. Therefore, God responded to Paul's prayer for healing deliverance with these words: "'My grace is sufficient for you, for my power is made perfect in weakness.' Therefore [Paul resolved] I will boast all the more gladly of my weaknesses, so that the power of Christ may rest upon me" (2 Corinthians 12:9–10).

You see, if we look at disability through the eyes of Christ, we will embrace human weakness as one means of making the strength of the Savior more glorious. We will see this not only individually, but corporately as churches. We will see disability as a means whereby Self may be further dethroned, not only in our individual hearts, but also in our local churches, as we practice the Savior's selfless love within the community of grace. We will also see disability ministry not as a separate ministry of the church, but as the normal work

24

of love within the family of God. In Christ there is no distinction. In Christ, whether "abled" or "dis-abled," the redeemed stand side by side as co-heirs with Christ, seated in the heavenly places with him (Ephesians 2:6). This realization promotes selfless love, which gives birth to a compassion that is far stronger than the kind of pity that even an unbeliever may feel. If human weakness enlarges the platform for the display of the strength and grace of the Savior, then we should welcome it. Let us not fear what God ordains for the sake of the greater glory of Christ!

Pillar #4:
Earthly Suffering Is Temporary and Designed to Shift Our Hope to Resurrection Glory

Jesus defined eternal life this way: "And this is eternal life, that they know you, the only true God, and Jesus Christ whom you have sent" (John 17:3). Possessing eternal life is not primarily about going to heaven when we die; it's a relationship with God that begins here—in this life—and continues for eternity. Eternal life begins at the moment we put saving faith in Jesus Christ as the one Mediator between God and man (1 Timothy 2:5), and it continues in a growing intimacy with our Savior in the here and now.

God's greater purpose for disability includes the immeasurable value of knowing Jesus Christ, which comes through sharing his sufferings. The apostle Paul rested in the righteousness of Christ as the basis of his being accepted by God (Philippians 3:8–10). However, he did not believe this was the extent of knowing God. Instead, his longing was "that I may know him and the power of his resurrection, and may share his sufferings, becoming like him in his death" (3:10). The word "know" here means to know personally, by experience. It denotes personal relationship. Thus *knowing Christ* is not merely aided by suffering, but requires it. Knowing Christ is *becoming like Christ* in his death, in anticipation of our future glory at the resurrection.

We may conclude, then, that suffering is a means of cultivating deeper fellowship with the Savior. Suffering contains unmatched sanctifying power for the believer, its larger purpose being to prepare us for a future glory that is far greater (weightier) and eternal. "So we do not lose heart. Though our outer self is wasting away, our inner self is being renewed day by day. For this light momentary affliction is preparing for us an eternal weight of glory beyond all comparison" (2 Corinthians 4:16–17).

Randy Alcorn is correct when he writes, "Paul insists that our sufferings will result in our greater good—God's people will be better off eternally because they suffer temporarily. From Paul's perspective, this trade-off will in eternity prove to be a great bargain."[13]

In disability, the heart of man becomes tethered to pain, thereby providing an opportunity for faith to be trained to be dependent upon the Lord. This, in turn, engenders a longing for the glory of our resurrection body, as the apostle says: "For I consider that the sufferings of this present time are not worth comparing with the glory that is to be revealed to us" (Romans 8:18). We could say it another way: without earthly suffering, no comparison would exist to point us to the eternal glory that awaits us in Christ. Thus these pillars of divine truth support the weightiest, most important goal of all: the glory of God.

## To the Praise of God's Glorious Grace
(All Things Are *to* God)

As stated at the beginning of this chapter, the glory of God is the beginning and end of all things. That is why the apostle closed the theological portion of the book of Romans with the doxological climax "For from him and through him and to him are all things. To him be glory forever. Amen" (Romans 11:36). Here the apostle is speaking of God as "the Originator, the Sustainer, and the Goal of all creation. *All things* means the totality. . . . He ascribes to God not simply 'glory,' but 'the glory.' Supreme glory belongs to God."[14]

God's greater purpose in all things, including disability, is to make known the glory of his grace, which is made visible through the person and work of his Son, Jesus Christ. In Ephesians 1:11, the apostle boldly declares that God "works all things according to the counsel of his will." All three members of the Trinity work in concert to accomplish redemption. The Father initiated the plan, the Son paid the price, and the Spirit applies redemption to the hearts and minds of sinners. And three times, in one long sentence, the apostle says God's redemptive work on behalf of sinners is "to the praise of his glorious grace" (Ephesians 1:6, 12, 14).

According to the Word of God, the eternal purposes of God will be accomplished "so that in the coming ages he might show the immeasurable riches of his grace in kindness toward us in Christ Jesus" (Ephesians 2:7). In the accomplishment of our redemption God displays attributes that would otherwise remain hidden—predominantly love, grace, and mercy toward sinners. In his divine wisdom, disability can be accepted as a gift from the Lord—one means by which his name may be glorified. He is the Strong One. He is the Helper. He is the Redeemer and Father of all who come to him through the Lord Jesus Christ.

*From Joni's Heart . . .*

Ask my husband: I am no theologian. I've never read Calvin's *Institutes* all the way through, nor do I know Greek or Hebrew. But decades ago, when I snapped my neck under the weight of a dive into shallow water, my paralysis pressed me up against a few big questions for God.

Up until then, I was content to wade ankle-deep in the shallow things of God, but when my body was left limp and useless, I was cast into the ocean. In the wee, sleepless hours I asked, God, when this broken neck happened, who was behind it? You or the devil? Are you permitting this or ordaining it? I'm still a young Christian . . if you're so loving, why treat your children so mean?

That was over fifty years ago.

Not once in those years has God been mean. What's more, he has satisfied my questions with an intimacy, softness, and sweetness of fellowship with him that I wouldn't trade for anything. Not even walking.

To me, the best of comforts is knowing that my life is nestled safely under God's overarching decrees. To be sure, when accidents happen, it's OK to call them accidents. Even the Bible does. When babies die, when whole populations starve, when young girls break their necks, God weeps for his world "for he does not afflict from his heart or grieve the children of men" (Lamentations 3:33). My spinal cord injury was a terrible accident. And so is the botched surgery that left your child brain-damaged, or the bus accident that left him or her with a life of chronic pain.

When all these things happen—when famines and crib deaths occur, when snakebites, gas station robberies, and pistol-whippings happen—God has not taken his hands off the wheel, not even for a nanosecond. As this chapter makes clear, God takes no delight in misery. But he is determined to steer suffering and use it for his own ends.

And those ends are happy. God is heaven-bent on sharing his joy with us. But there's a catch: God shares his joy on his terms. And those terms call for us to, in some measure, suffer as his beloved Son did while on earth. When suffering sandblasts you to the core, the true stuff of which you are made is revealed—and often, it's not very pretty. Suffering rips away the veneer so that we can be better bonded to the Savior.

Does this mean God is happy about my spinal cord injury? Was he delighted and rubbing his hands in glee when I dove off the raft into shallow water? Of course not. He may work "all things" together for my good, but that does not mean a terrible accident is a good thing (Romans 8:28). God permits all sorts of things he doesn't approve of. But as I often say, he permits things he hates in order to accomplish things he loves—and that's Christ in us, the hope of glory.

I'm not about to waste my quadriplegia. This broken earth provides my one and only chance to show that I can trust God in my hardships. By God's grace, I'll keep doing it until finally God closes the curtain on suffering and all its sorrow. And I hope you join me in the same.

*Joni*
———

# Chapter 2

# Where Is God in Our Suffering?

*But the LORD was with Joseph and showed him*
*steadfast love.*

(Genesis 39:21)

*As for you, you meant evil against me, but God*
*meant it for good, to bring it about that many*
*people should be kept alive, as they are today.*

(Genesis 50:20)

When we look at our troubles it's easy to wonder if God is really in control or if even he can bring good out of all the bad things that happen. But as we willingly place our minds under the authority of Scripture, we begin to see things from God's perspective. He is always at work on behalf of those whom he loves. He is always up to something good and is working out a bigger plan. This is true even when disability hits home.

God knows that our spiritual sight is limited and that we have a hard time understanding what he is doing through human suffering. How good it is, then, that the Holy Spirit included a remarkable story of God's providence in Scripture.

The providence of God, as explained in the previous chapter, means that God uses his infinite power and wisdom to continuously preserve and guide every part of his creation toward his good purpose. Providence assures us that not only is God working out his master plan for the universe, but he is also at work carrying out his will for our good and his glory. This also means that God is not far away, but is always present, near, and attentive to all of our ways and needs. Jesus says it this way:

31

"Are not five sparrows sold for two pennies? And not one of them is forgotten before God. Why, even the hairs of your head are all numbered. Fear not; you are of more value than many sparrows" (Luke 12:6–8).

Think of it: God knows even the number of hairs on your head! That is Jesus' way of saying that God is intimately acquainted with everything that is going on in our lives. Consider how the psalmist says the same:

> *Upon you I have leaned from before my birth;*
> *you are he who took me from my mother's womb.*
> *My praise is continually of you.*
>
> (Psalm 71:6)

In his gracious providence, God constantly works out his will according to his perfect timing: "For everything there is a season, and a time for every matter under heaven" (Ecclesiastes 3:1). God's timing is always precise. He's never a day too early or late. This should bring us great comfort in times of uncertainty and affliction.

One of the most powerful stories of God guiding all things toward the fulfillment of his promised redemption is that of the life and trials of Joseph recorded in the book of Genesis, chapters 37–50. Joseph experienced his share of trouble and yet his life was filled with what some would think to be mere "coincidences" if they did not so unmistakably demonstrate the loving care of divine providence.

The New Testament book of Acts provides a fitting summary of the life of Joseph. When Stephen, a leader in the church at Jerusalem, was hauled before the civil authorities and falsely accused, he seized the opportunity for God's glory. Boldly, he preached a long view of the gospel—that is, the big picture of God's rescue plan for the Hebrew people, and, through them, the hope of salvation for all mankind:

> *And the patriarchs, jealous of Joseph, sold him into*
> *Egypt; but God was with him and rescued him*

*out of all his afflictions and gave him favor and*
*wisdom before Pharaoh, king of Egypt, who made*
*him ruler over Egypt and over all his household.*
*Now there came a famine throughout all Egypt*
*and Canaan, and great affliction, and our fathers*
*could find no food. But when Jacob heard that*
*there was grain in Egypt, he sent out our fathers*
*on their first visit. And on the second visit Joseph*
*made himself known to his brothers, and Joseph's*
*family became known to Pharaoh. And Joseph*
*sent and summoned Jacob his father and all his*
*kindred, seventy-five persons in all. And Jacob*
*went down into Egypt, and he died, he and our*
*fathers, and they were carried back to Shechem*
*and laid in the tomb that Abraham had bought*
*for a sum of silver from the sons of Hamor in*
*Shechem.*

*But as the time of the promise drew near,*
*which God had granted to Abraham, the people*
*increased and multiplied in Egypt until there arose*
*over Egypt another king who did not know Joseph.*

(Acts 7:9–18)

In his providence, God utilized the evil that Joseph's brothers committed against him, in order to move him to Egypt. While Joseph was there, God gave him wisdom and leadership beyond his years, in order to prevent his family and many others from starving to death. Not only were the immediate descendants of Abraham saved from starvation through the afflictions of Joseph, but, more importantly, the earthly line of the Messiah was preserved. If God had not caused Joseph to endure his afflictions then Abraham's family would have perished and God's promise would have died with Joseph. But God is not one to let his promises perish. Instead, he carried out his master plan, while also being attentive to all that was going on in Joseph's life.

In the outworking of both the trials and the triumphs of

Joseph, we see the unfolding of a beautifully woven tapestry of sovereign grace, wisdom, and goodness. Here we glean several truths which can strengthen your faith in God's providence, no matter what suffering you may now face.

## God's Providence Assures Us of His Presence, Even When Bad Things Happen to Us

The summary of Joseph's life, which Stephen gives, includes various kinds of affliction. According to Genesis 37, these trials began when Joseph was seventeen years old, when he (the tattletale of the family) repeatedly brought a bad report about his brothers to his dad (Genesis 37:1–4). Not surprisingly, this behavior, along with his father's favoritism (through the giving of a special multicolored coat), provoked Joseph's brothers to hatred and jealousy. A little later, Joseph told them about two dreams he had had, which predicted his exaltation over his brothers and parents. This drove the wedge even deeper. Consequently, his brothers began to plot against him. "Let's get rid of that dreamer," they said (see 37:5–20).

Sold into slavery by his brothers, presumed dead by his father, taken to a foreign land, falsely accused, and eventually thrown into prison, Joseph may have been tempted to think that God had forgotten or forsaken him (37:21–35; 39:19–20). But that was not the case. Repeatedly, the Scripture assures us that God was always present, saying that "the LORD was with Joseph" (39:2–3, 21–23). Whatever Joseph did the Lord made to succeed, because God was *with* him.

Further testimony to the gracious providence of God is Joseph's naming of his sons. He named his firstborn Manasseh, for, he said, "God has made me forget all my hardship and all my father's house." He named his second son Ephraim, "For God has made me fruitful in the land of my affliction" (41:51–52). God was faithfully working in, through, and behind the scenes, while innumerable and unexplainable trials were going on in Joseph's life. God was always present. At every moment, God was compassionately attentive to Joseph's suffering. The same is true for you and me.

## God's Providence Includes Larger, Redemptive Purposes for Our Suffering

Understanding the purpose of God in our suffering can be like trying to assemble a jigsaw puzzle without the picture on the box. But God always has a larger plan which we cannot see, a plan that involves more—but never less—than trials and blessings. He knows our every need, and he leads and guides us faithfully. For example, in Genesis 42–44, the dreams that Joseph had were fulfilled when he was thirty-nine years old (twenty-two years after his first dream). God gave Joseph the ability to interpret Pharaoh's dreams, and the wisdom to fill storehouses with grain so that one day he could sell it in exchange for land.

When famine brought Joseph's brothers to Egypt to buy grain, Joseph had numerous interactions with them. Finally, his emotions couldn't be contained any longer, and he revealed himself to them. He wept so loudly that even the Egyptians in the house of Pharaoh could hear him (45:2). Twenty-two years of bottled-up emotions, and Joseph comes face to face with his abusers: his own brothers who had betrayed and forsaken him. He wept. But God's grace did not only extend to Joseph; through him, it reached out to his brothers as well.

"I am Joseph!" he said to his brothers (45:3). Then he added:

*"Come near to me, please." And they came near.*
*And he said, "I am your brother, Joseph, whom you*
*sold into Egypt. And now do not be distressed or*
*angry with yourselves because you sold me here,*
*for God sent me before you to preserve life. For*
*the famine has been in the land these two years,*
*and there are yet five years in which there will be*
*neither plowing nor harvest. And God sent me*
*before you to preserve for you a remnant on earth*
*and to keep alive for you many survivors."*
*(Genesis 45:4–7)*

Don't miss this. Twice Joseph acknowledged that it was God who had sent him into Egypt. "*You* sold me, but *God* sent me" is essentially what he said. So Joseph sent his brothers back to Canaan to retrieve their father and their belongings (45:1–15). When they arrived, Pharaoh settled them in the best land in Egypt (47:1–6). As the famine continued, Joseph purchased all the land in exchange for grain, thus making Pharaoh the owner of all real estate in Egypt. As the book of Genesis draws to an end, Jacob meets his grandsons, Joseph's sons, and blesses them (Genesis 48). He then blesses and charges his own twelve sons, and dies (Genesis 49).

Then comes the finale, the declaration of God's absolute sovereignty over all, and the intricate outworking of his providence: "As for you," Joseph said to his brothers, "you meant evil against me, but God meant it for good, to bring it about that many people should be kept alive, as they are today" (50:20). The New Testament affirms the same truth, but in a slightly different way: "we know that for those who love God all things work together for good, for those who are called according to his purpose" (Romans 8:28). If you are a follower of Christ, you can be confident that, even in the midst of difficult trials, God will not waste any of your pain. He will graciously use it to move closer to the goal of molding you into the image of Jesus (Romans 8:29).

## God's Providence Enables Us to Accept Our Limitations

When Joseph returned to Egypt after burying his father, his brothers became afraid, saying, "It may be that Joseph will hate us and pay us back for all the evil that we did to him" (50:15). So they slipped back into their deceptive ways by claiming that their father had commanded them to tell Joseph to forgive all the evils they had committed against him (50:16–17). But this was not necessary, since God's grace had gripped Joseph's heart. "Do not fear," he said, "for am I in the place of God?" Joseph understood that ultimately the punishment of those who had hurt him belonged exclusively in the hands of one person, and it wasn't him; it was God. In other words, Joseph knew his place, because he knew God's place.

Sometimes suffering enters our lives as the result of the mistakes or intentional wrongdoing of others. When this is the case we need to humbly accept what God allows, since he is the only one who knows every detail of every situation. God is the one to whom we can fully entrust any injustice. In this way, Joseph was like Jesus, who did not pay back evil for evil because he entrusted his unjust affliction to the Father who will one day judge all (1 Peter 2:23).

In an emotional moment, Joseph didn't excuse his brothers' sin. He accepted that their motives and actions were wicked, but that God's higher purpose reigned over all: "As for you, you meant evil against me, but God meant it for good, to bring it about that many people should be kept alive, as they are today" (Genesis 50:20). The same tension between the actions of men and the sovereignty of God existed at the crucifixion of Jesus. In his sermon on the day of Pentecost, Peter rightly accused the Jewish leaders of murdering Jesus. Yet he also said that what they had done was "according to the predetermined plan and foreknowledge of God" (Acts 2:23 NASB). It was the predetermined plan that the Son of God was slain before the foundation of the world to pay for our sins. Yet God held those who crucified Jesus fully responsible. God's grace triumphed over evil. He brought about immeasurable good through what was surely the most horrific suffering any man has ever experienced on earth.

When the opportunity to exact revenge arose, Joseph comforted his brothers instead and spoke kindly to them. Joseph's words of grace continued until the day of his death in Egypt, at 110 years old.

*Joseph saw Ephraim's children of the third generation. The children also of Machir the son of Manasseh were counted as Joseph's own. And*

*Joseph said to his brothers, "I am about to die,
but God will visit you and bring you up out of this
land to the land that he swore to Abraham, to
Isaac, and to Jacob." Then Joseph made the sons of
Israel swear, saying, "God will surely visit you, and
you shall carry up my bones from here." So Joseph
died, being 110 years old. They embalmed him,
and he was put in a coffin in Egypt.*

(Genesis 50:23–26)

Joseph made the sons of Israel promise to someday carry his bones to the Promised Land, because he believed the promise made to Abraham that, after four hundred years of slavery in Egypt, God would deliver his people (Genesis 15:13–14). By saying "you shall carry up my bones from here," Joseph demonstrated that his faith was alive. One day, he would receive a reward for believing that, somehow, behind the scenes of his life's drama, God had been providentially at work. All along, God had been bringing Joseph to where he needed to be at exactly the right moment in time, so that God's greater plan would continue to unfold.

The life of Joseph brings massive encouragement to our hearts, because through it we witness the kind providence of God. When suffering hits home, we may not understand God's specific intentions. However, we do know this: God is near. He is attentive. He walks through our valleys of suffering with us and is moving all things toward the goal of his glory; and what is for God's glory turns out to also be for our good. He is worthy of our trust.

## *From Joni's Heart . . .*

On a warm summer morning, April and her husband loaded their boys into the SUV for a week of camping in the Sierras. Halfway there, April unsnapped her shoulder harness and leaned over the seat to open the cooler. At that moment, an oncoming car suddenly crossed in front of their vehicle to turn into a rest area. There was no time to brake. Their SUV slammed into the car, injuring the elderly driver and killing his passenger. April was thrown against the dashboard. The impact snapped her neck.

That was fifteen years ago. When I met April, she was slumped in her wheelchair, a quadriplegic sitting in occupational therapy, weeping bitterly. Her OT's advice seemed to be falling on deaf ears. So, I parked my wheelchair next to her and I cried, too.

My tears flowed from the deepest parts of a fellow sufferer. I knew firsthand the horrors April was facing, and I silently pleaded, *Oh, God, how will this young mother ever make it? How can I comfort her?* April had reason to cry. Within a year, her husband would leave her, plummeting her into a custody battle that only made things more unbearable.

When things like this happen, there are no answers. At least, not initially. April was like a little girl who rode a bike too fast, crashed to the asphalt, and ended up with a bloody knee, crying "Why?" to her daddy running up. The child is not so much looking for answers as wanting Daddy to wipe her knee, pick her up, pat her on the back, and assure her, saying, "There, there, sweetheart; it's OK, Daddy's here."

That was the fundamental cry of April's heart. It's our cry, too. Jesus, the Man of Sorrows, is the Bread of Life, torn and broken for the nourishment of people like us. As someone wrote, "Sorrow is like a knife that cuts gaps and openings in our hearts through which our Savior may more easily enter." When he does, we discover that he himself is the Answer.

Looking back, April was comforted when she finally saw the bigger picture. Joseph, who suffered through betrayal, slavery, and imprisonment, had the big picture when he said to his wicked brothers, "You intended to harm me, but God intended it for good to accomplish what is now being done, *the saving of many lives*" (Genesis 50:20 NIV). Over time, April came to see how her life was for "the saving of many lives." Her life was a stage on which God was acting out his grace, all for the benefit of an audience inspired by her perseverance. Once she saw how high the cosmic stakes were, it invigorated her faith.

Think of Joseph and April. Look at the times you survived your own suffering in years past: did your perseverance influence others around you, showcasing to them the saving power of God? Paul meant exactly this in 2 Corinthians 1:6: "If we are afflicted, it is for your comfort and salvation."

Just recently, April passed away from complications connected to her disability.

At her funeral, after the last person spoke, I wheeled up front and said, near to tears, "Knowing firsthand what April had to go through every morning just to sit up in her wheelchair . . . well, it comforts me even now in my own affliction. Her simple act of 'facing the day' inspires me to do the same." That morning, I venture to say my hard-fought-for confession comforted many in the congregation.

And so, comfort received in suffering is passed on. Whether you've struggled through a broken ankle, home, or neck, you are not allowed to sit on the sidelines, resting on the comfort God imparted when you were at your lowest. You have received God's consolations, and, that being so, more is expected of you. Your next go-round with affliction will be God's tap on your shoulder to find those who are hurting more than you, so that you can enable them to deal with their sorrow. Help make them brave.

It's what broken people do with broken bread.

*Joni*

# Chapter 3

# What Is God Doing through Disability?

*As he passed by, he saw a man blind from birth. And his disciples asked him, "Rabbi, who sinned, this man or his parents, that he was born blind?" Jesus answered, "It was not that this man sinned, or his parents, but that the works of God might be displayed in him."*

(John 9:1–3)

In Ephesians 1:11, the apostle Paul boldly asserts that God "works *all things* according to the counsel of his will." This statement is in the middle of the longest sentence in the Greek New Testament, which covers twelve verses in our English Bible. As we noted earlier, three times in this one long sentence it is made clear that God's redemptive work is "to the praise of his glorious grace" (1:6, 12, 14). In other words, the eternal purposes of God are accomplished "so that in the coming ages he might show the immeasurable riches of his grace in kindness toward us in Christ Jesus" (2:7). By redeeming sinners through the Son of God's saving work, God displays attributes that would otherwise remain hidden—predominantly his grace toward sinners.

This means that God's greater purpose in all things—including disability—is to make known the glory of his grace which is made visible through the person and work of his Son, Jesus Christ. This is powerfully illustrated in the Gospel of John, where we see the Savior compassionately heal a man of his physical affliction. However, we also see the Savior extend saving grace to save the man's soul and give him eternal life.

The ninth chapter of the Gospel of John gives birth to God-centered hope by shedding light on some very important truths God wants us to understand and embrace. Here is an amazing record of God's kindness toward a blind man who had never even seen a single sunrise or sunset, the faces of his parents, or even the food he put into his mouth. Imagine sitting by the roadside, unnoticed, listening to the sound of thousands of people walking by you each day.

The foremost question in the disciples' minds, "Who sinned?," reveals thoughts that often nag us, but in the compassion of Jesus we see some reasons why God allows pain and suffering in our world. Most importantly, this account of Jesus healing a blind man shines a floodlight of truth into our spiritual darkness. Eternal hope was born as the man's eyes were opened by Jesus.

## God Has Glorious Purposes for Disability

The first verse of John 9 mentions that as Jesus passed by "he saw a man blind from birth." Jesus *saw*. This needy man did not escape the notice of the Savior. Jesus did not keep his eyes focused only ahead of him, or look the other way, or move to the other side of the road (as the priest and Levite did to the beaten man in the story of the Good Samaritan in Luke 10:25–37). No, Jesus *saw* the blind man, a priceless creation made in God's image. However, the disciples (like us at times) only saw a problem. But as Jesus passed by, a teaching moment was set up. So the disciples opened class by asking a question: "Rabbi, who sinned, this man or his parents, that he was born blind?" (9:2).

Who sinned? In the minds of the disciples, that was the only question. Someone *had* to have sinned. There was simply no other explanation for the man's blindness, or so the disciples thought. "Sin, either in the parents or in the child, must be the cause," they thought. At least one of the three must be guilty. "Which is it, Jesus? Is it him or his parents? Or is there some kind of generational, family sin that has cursed him?"

44

Exactly *how* this man would have been able to sin before he was born is not explained, but the disciples asked the question anyway. Or could it have been his parents? Perhaps the disciples were prompted by their remembrance of Exodus 20:5, where Moses warns the people of Israel that God visits "the iniquity of the fathers on the children to the third and the fourth generation." Maybe that verse was floating around in their heads. Whatever the reasons behind their question, in their minds *every* disability must have a specific sin cause.

Now, there is an ounce of truth in this connection, but there is also a gallon of error. Let me explain.

Every form of pain and suffering is the result of the original curse pronounced on mankind by God after sin entered the world (Genesis 3:14–19). The world was once perfect, but it's not like that anymore. Instead, we live in a fallen world. So, in a generic sense, there is a connection between sin and suffering.

For the Christian, too, there may indeed be times when there is a specific connection between suffering and sin, as God sometimes allows us to reap the consequences of our disobedience. However, this is part of the outworking of God's chastening love; it is not punishment. The Bible teaches that Jesus, the Lamb of God, took the punishment for our sins (1 Peter 3:18). When we place our faith in Jesus as Savior and Lord, the heavenly Father adopts us into his family. As children of God, we are loved so much that God will discipline us for our good, so that we are trained in righteousness (Hebrews 12:3–11).[15] This was not the case with the blind man.

So that is the ounce of truth. However, the gallon of error that washed over the disciples' thinking was that there is *always* a connection between *personal* suffering and *personal* sin. That was their chief error.

"Who sinned, Jesus?" they asked. But Jesus answers them in an unexpected way. "Neither" is his reply. "It was not that this man sinned, or his parents" (John 9:3). Neither the man nor his parents were the cause of his blindness. The man and his parents were sinners: Jesus does not deny that. Nonetheless,

Jesus eliminates a personal connection between their sinfulness and the man's blindness. Rather, the man was born blind so "that the works of God might be displayed in him" (9:4). This was a shocking statement!

The Judaism of that day resisted the idea that God could be responsible for letting an innocent person suffer. But Jesus makes no attempt to get God off the hook. Instead, he makes it clear that the man's blindness fits perfectly into God's sovereign plan. Clearly, the governing force behind this man's disability was not any one person's sin, but God's larger agenda to display his work and the glory of his grace.

*We must not miss this!*

Herein lies the fundamental purpose of disability: to draw attention to God! Physical and intellectual disabilities are God-ordained means of displaying his wisdom and power. They are his way of shifting our earthbound focus from temporal comforts to what is infinitely more valuable in light of eternity. Jesus makes it crystal clear that this man was born blind *on purpose*—that is, according to the purposes of God.

## God-Glorifying Works

Jesus continues, "I must work the works of Him who sent Me" (9:4 NKJV). Obviously, one of the works which Jesus was sent to accomplish was to give sight to *this* blind man on *this* day, while declaring, "I am the light of the world" (9:5). William MacDonald comments, "Before the man was born, the Lord Jesus knew He would give sight to those blind eyes."[16]

This specific work brought glory to God: "I must do God-glorifying works as long as it is day," according to Jesus, as long as there was opportunity. For "the night is coming"—that is, Jesus' death was near (when his work would be complete). The death of Jesus on the cross for man's sin, followed by his victorious resurrection, would be his greatest work. When that work was finished and he ascended into heaven, he was done. He would sit down at the right hand of God (Mark 16:19). But for now, his attention was on this one blind man. How comforting this is!

Notice the compassion that Jesus displayed toward him. It should both astonish and rebuke us. To the disciples, this man was someone to be talked *about*, not *to*. They introduced him as "this man," as if he didn't have a name, and spoke about him in the third person, as if he wasn't sitting right there listening to their every word. He was a bothersome conundrum. "What's wrong with him?" "Why is he blind?" "Whose fault is it?" "Why has God allowed this to happen?" In the moment, their questions were more important than the needy man himself. In contrast, Jesus views the blind man as a priceless image-bearer of God, and goes straight toward him. He talks *to* him, not *about* him. Jesus sees him in his neediness, and reaches out in mercy and love. There is so much application here for us, even if we do not personally suffer with disabilities. By placing people affected by disability into our lives, the Lord gives us opportunities to display impartial, living faith.

Another clear example of the sovereignty of God over disability and the work of healing is the account of the healing at the pool of Bethesda (John 5:1–17). Though John informs us that there was "a multitude of invalids—blind, lame, and paralyzed" lying beside the pool, Jesus chose to heal only one man out of them all. By doing so, Jesus again demonstrated that he was working alongside the Father according to his will (John 5:17).

## The Human Touch

We might wonder, "Why dirt? Why mud?" (John 9:6). MacDonald writes, "Some have suggested that the man had no eyeballs and that the Lord Jesus simply created them at that moment. Others suggest that in giving sight to the blind, the Lord Jesus commonly used methods that were despised in the eyes of the world. He used weak and insignificant things in working out His purposes."[17] However, I see no reason to read more into the Scriptures than is plainly there. Certainly Jesus could have done anything. According to Genesis 2:7, the Lord "formed . . . man of dust from the ground." In this case, however, Jesus spit on the ground, and mixed his saliva into the dirt. Then he spread it over the man's eyes as a clay paste and commanded him to go wash it off.

However, there is a more important question than "Why the dirt?," namely, "Why the human touch?" Why didn't Jesus just say something like "Eyes, open!"? The reason is that the human touch is an expression of compassion, care, and tenderness. It communicates that Jesus was not afraid of being contaminated by this less-than-typical man, as he touched the very wound which would have been viewed as unclean. Think about it. Here is the personal touch of God in the flesh out of compassion for a blind man. Here is a nonverbal expression of love, care, acceptance, and value. How kind it was for Jesus to touch this socially deprived man!

We can learn so much from how Jesus treated this lonely man, since one of the biggest challenges people with disabilities face is isolation. Lack of acceptance often leads to deep feelings of loneliness. But what an honor it is for us to extend the grace of Christ in a way that says, "You are important. You are made in a special way, according to God's image. God knows your situation and he loves you. I love you, and am so glad you're here. We want you to be part of our church family." The tenderness of Jesus is an example for us to follow.

Jesus said, "'Go, wash in the pool of Siloam' (which means Sent)." Why did Jesus heal the man this way? To demonstrate the obedience of faith. Jesus knew this man had an eternally more serious disability, which Jesus was going to heal. The blind man was called to simply obey the words of Jesus, to obey the command of a man whom he had never seen. You see, there was something more important going on in this man's heart. He was beginning to take God at his word, though he did not yet know who Jesus really was. But as he made his way to the pool to wash his eyes, his blindness of heart was lifted by the Spirit of God, and he "came back seeing."

Immediately, his neighbors took notice and some asked, "Could it really be him?" (see 9:8), while others said, "Well, he's kind of like him" (9:9). But then he spoke up for himself: "I am the man." His testimony can be summed up in three words: "Jesus did it." Those who heard asked, "Where is [Jesus]?" "I do not know" was the man's reply, since he had not yet seen Jesus.

## Man's Greatest Disability Is Spiritual

The second important truth we learn from John 9 is that Jesus' primary purpose for coming to earth was to meet our deepest need, which is spiritual, not physical. The neighbors brought the man to the Pharisees (John 9:13), undoubtedly because Jesus' good deed had been performed on a Sabbath. The people feared the religious leaders more than they feared God, and did not want to be in disfavor with those who considered it work to make clay on a Sabbath, even if it was part of a miraculous healing. The rest of the chapter contains the tiresome dialogue that took place between the Pharisees, the man, and his parents.

First, the Pharisees questioned the formerly blind man. But they had a dilemma. Is the miracle worker a sinner or a saint? The Pharisees have to say that Jesus is a sinner because, in their mind, any truly God-fearing man would not have helped another human being on a Sabbath day. However, the healed man said, "He is a prophet" (9:17). Next, the Pharisees interrogate the man's parents, since the Jews "did not believe" he had actually been healed (9:18). So they posed two questions to the man's parents: Is this your son, who you say was born blind? And how can he now see?

His parents answered the first question, but deferred the second to their son: "Ask him; he is of age. He will speak for himself" (9:21). John tells us why they answered in this way: it was through fear of the religious leaders (9:22).

So the Pharisees interrogated the healed man a second time (9:24–34). At this point, the Pharisees were coming unglued. Their hardened hearts refused to accept the truth about Jesus. So they turned to personal attack, as spiritual pride oozed out of them, saying, "You are his disciple, but we are disciples of Moses" (9:28).

The defiance of the Pharisees opened a door for the man to give witness about Jesus for a third time. Finally, when the religious hypocrites couldn't take it anymore, they put the man out of the synagogue. They excommunicated him. Now the man has been rejected twice: first, when he was blind, and now, when he sees. What irony to receive this kind of treatment from those who claimed to know God!

## Jesus Heals Our Greatest Disability

In this account of Jesus' healing we see blindness removed twice. Not only did Jesus stop walking and heal the man, but he also took initiative to seek out the rejected man and perform a more important miracle. The greater miracle was the removal of spiritual blindness by the giving of spiritual light. "Lord, I believe," said the man (9:39). The blindness of the man's heart was now removed, and he worshipped Jesus. Once ostracized and alone, this man was now part of God's family. What a glorious miracle!

However, unbelief is not always cured; not every person receives Jesus for who he really is. Jesus makes this clear when he speaks to the formerly blind man, but in a public place: "For judgment I came into this world." By saying this, Jesus is not contradicting John 3:17, "For God did not send the Son into the world to judge the world, but that the world might be saved through Him" (NASB). He is merely testifying that every encounter that he has with a person draws a line in the sand. Each and every person is accountable for how they respond to Jesus. While Jesus brings sight to those who know they are spiritually blind, he also blinds those who already think they can see.

Every sinner responds to the light of Jesus in one of two ways: aware of their blindness, they welcome and embrace him as the Light of the World, or, filled with self-righteous pride, they reject him (John 1:11–12). Those who are convinced they already possess spiritual sight harden their hearts and confirm their blindness.

Some of the Pharisees overheard Jesus speak to the man, which, of course, was the Savior's intention. "Are we also blind?" they asked (John 9:40). Jesus answered, "If you were blind, you would have no guilt" (9:41). In other words, if they would humbly admit their blindness, they would demonstrate they were the kind of people whom God forgives. Disability reminds us that every one of us is spiritually helpless, unable to come to God on our own. But the grace of God has come to us in Jesus. Consequently, we must humble ourselves before God, admit that we are spiritually blinded by sin, and embrace by faith the One who said, "I am the light of the world. Whoever follows me will not walk in darkness, but will have the light of life" (8:12).

In God's sight, we are all disabled. Every human being is blind, deaf, and cognitively disabled to some degree. All of us have been negatively impacted by the fall of man from his original glory, and each of us continues to fall short of the glory of God (Romans 3:23). As a result, *inability* is our greatest disability, and it was this which Jesus Christ came to cure. Every human being's greatest need, whether "abled" or "dis-abled," is for the grace of God to overcome our spiritual disabilities. This is why Jesus came to earth.

The Gospel of Luke informs us that when Jesus came to his hometown of Nazareth,

> *he went to the synagogue on the Sabbath day, and he stood up to read. And the scroll of the prophet Isaiah was given to him. He unrolled the scroll and found the place where it was written,*
>
> *"The Spirit of the Lord is upon me,*
> *because he has anointed me*
> *to proclaim good news to the poor.*
> *He has sent me to proclaim liberty to the captives*
> *and recovering of sight to the blind,*
> *to set at liberty those who are oppressed,*
> *to proclaim the year of the Lord's favor."*
>
> *And he rolled up the scroll and gave it back to the attendant and sat down. And the eyes of all in the synagogue were fixed on him. And he began to say to them, "Today this Scripture has been fulfilled in your hearing."*
>
> (Luke 4:16–21)

Seven hundred years before Jesus was born, Isaiah predicted that Messiah would preach the gospel to the poor, proclaim release to the captives, give sight to the blind, and set free the oppressed. Yet Jesus did not come for the physically poor (Matthew 26:11). He did not come for the physically blind. He did not come for those who live in brick-and-mortar prisons. No, he came for those who are *spiritually* poor: bankrupt, without any spiritual riches. He came to set free those who are held captive in the prison of sin. He came to open the eyes of the blinded heart. He came to unlock our sin-oppressed souls. He came for us! Because of the sin nature we inherited from Adam, all of us are blind to the glory and goodness of God. We are all deaf to his Word. We are all intellectually challenged (Ephesians 4:18). Only through the new birth and illumination of the Holy Spirit can we have the spiritual mind to comprehend and appreciate the truth that is in Jesus Christ. We are helpless, as Romans 5:6 states: "For while we were still helpless, at the appointed moment, Christ died for the ungodly" (HCSB).

Now, because of the gracious work of Jesus on the cross, God calls each of us to turn away from any confidence in our own ability to meet his righteous requirements, and to turn in faith toward the One who has already met them on our behalf. Jesus offered his sinless life on the cross in our place, as the sin-atoning sacrifice that every sinner needs. Three days later, God victoriously raised his Son from the dead to declare that sinners may now come to him through repentance and faith. Therefore, God now offers forgiveness, salvation, and eternal life to all who will come to him, who will rest their dependence upon the finished work of Jesus (Romans 10:9–10; 2 Corinthians 5:21; Matthew 10:28–30).

Physical and intellectual disabilities remind us of the greater disability we have all been afflicted with through our genetic link to Adam. Apart from the gospel, we are forever disabled, but there is hope in Christ. The gospel replaces our spiritual bankruptcy with the immeasurable riches of Jesus (Ephesians 2:7), removes the scales from the eyes of our hearts, thus enabling us to see the glory of Jesus (2 Corinthians 3:1–18), and sets us free from spiritual imprisonment and oppression (Romans 6:5–8).

## "At the End of That Hallway"

As I mentioned in the Introduction, it was while attending a conference in Chicago in April 2011 that the Lord gave me a new friend, John, who is the father of Paul, who was born without eyes. Now an adult, Paul still weighs less than 100 pounds, due to growth hormone deficiency, and suffers from multiple disorders on the autism spectrum. And this is just the tip of the iceberg of Paul's disabilities.

We can only imagine what it was like for John, a first-time dad, to hold his newly born son. "It was thrilling," John said, "for about fifteen seconds." Then the news of Paul's blindness was brought to his parents, and they were never the same. In response to the news, John reacted in great anger. He declared that God was cruel. As a result, John and his wife left their church. Over a period of almost two years, however, God used the tender, persistent love of church members to soften John's cold, bitter, and calloused heart. The Holy Spirit revealed to him just how blind and sinful *he* was—that he was not truly a Christian as he had deceived himself into thinking he was. One day, as he walked down the hallway of a hospital in Indianapolis, God stopped John in his tracks and opened his spiritually blinded eyes. John said, "At the end of that hallway I knew I needed Jesus in a way I had never known."

Do you see how good and gracious God is? Do you see how God's purposes are greater and his ways higher than ours? From God's perspective, the blindness of John's spiritual heart was an eternally more serious problem than his son's empty eye sockets. Indeed, John was the one with the disability!

And that's the way it is for all of us.

According to God's infinite wisdom and unsearchable ways, disability may be seen as a gift from the Lord—a means by which his name may be glorified. Indeed, God is the strong one. He is our helper. He is the Redeemer and Savior of all who come to him by faith in Jesus Christ.

*From Joni's Heart . . .*

Everyone who takes the Bible seriously agrees that God hates suffering. Jesus even spent most of his time relieving it. The Bible tells us to feed the hungry, clothe the poor, visit prisoners, and speak up for the helpless. God cares about the needs of the afflicted.

When we feel compassion for people in distress, we know that God felt it first. And he shows this every day, even now, by raising sick people from their beds, sometimes to the wonder of doctors. Every day God grants childless couples babies, pulls depressed people out of the pits, protects Alzheimer's patients when they cross the street, and writes happy endings to sad situations. Even when he punishes sin, Ezekiel 18:32 says that it gives God no pleasure.

But it doesn't follow that God's only relationship to suffering is to relieve it. He specifically says that all who follow Jesus can expect hardship.

At first, it doesn't sound comforting to know that God has wired this world to be difficult. "Man is born to trouble as surely as sparks fly upward" (Job 5:7 NIV). Even the apostle Paul knew the importance of helping fellow believers grasp a rugged, realistic view of life. He was intent on "strengthening the disciples and encouraging them to remain true to the faith," telling them in the next breath, "We must go through many hardships to enter the kingdom of God" (Acts 14:22 NIV).

Even the Son of God states it plainly: "If anyone would come after me, let him deny himself and take up his cross and follow me. For whoever would save his life will lose it, but whoever loses his life for my sake will find it" (Matthew 16:24–25).

This is hard for people to hear. I certainly didn't like it when I broke my neck in a diving accident. Like most in similar situations, I wrestled against God, feeling as though he were unfair. After all, I was one of his children. Why would he treat me—treat any of his children—so harshly? My every prayer request revolved around making things "right" again. I wanted to walk. And Matthew 7:9–11 gave me every confidence that walking was a good request. There Jesus said, "Which of you, if your son asks for bread, will give him a stone? Or if he asks for a fish, will give him a snake? If you, then, though you are evil, know how to give good gifts to your children, how much more will your Father in heaven give good gifts to those who ask him!" (NIV).

What could be better than walking? Having use of my hands and legs would be such a good gift from my Father in heaven. It would be the "fair" thing for him to do!

You can imagine my disappointment when, several years later, I was still paralyzed. *God*, I thought, *you even say in Psalm 84:11 that you withhold no good thing from those whose walk is blameless. I'm not doing anything bad, so . . . isn't it time you gave me back the use of my legs?*

Then one day, a friend said, "Joni, I want you to know I think you're pretty courageous. I see your smile and it tells me that I can smile through my problems, too, by the grace of God." Her comment struck a chord. Something told me that this was God's good gift. It's good to be courageous in the face of trials. It's good to show patience during irritation. It's good to remain hopeful when all else appears dismal. These are good gifts—yet they are only realized in the hardships of life.

So how do we read Matthew 7:9–11? We may ask for financial stability, but God might give something better: a deeper, stronger faith. We may ask for a clean medical report, but God might give us a sweeter reliance on his grace. Some of God's best gifts must be unwrapped in the dark. Just consider Jesus' Beatitudes: happy are the poor in spirit . . . the meek . . . those who hunger and thirst . . . and those who mourn.

Why are these the happy ones? Because they are recipients of a peace that is profound and a joy that is unshakable. These are God's gifts. And so are faith, courage, perseverance, endurance, and more. God says in Jeremiah 32:41, "I will rejoice in doing them good . . . with all my heart and all my soul." So, ask yourself: "What 'good thing' has the Lord slipped into my hands during these difficult days of dealing with disability?"

*Joni*

# Chapter 4

# Does God Make Mistakes in the Womb?

*Your eyes saw my unformed substance;*
*And in Your book were all written*
*The days that were ordained for me,*
*When as yet there was not one of them.*

(Psalm 139:16 NASB)

While I was in the final stage of writing this book, our sixth grandchild was born. The thirty-one weeks of life she enjoyed in the safety of her mother's womb continued for only forty-five minutes after birth. Then she was immediately escorted into the arms of her Creator and Savior.

At eleven weeks' gestation, our daughter and son-in-law learned of their firstborn's dire medical complications—complications that would probably make it impossible for her to survive outside the womb. Medical personnel immediately offered them termination of pregnancy, but they responded that since they knew their little girl was created in the image of God, that wasn't an option to consider.

As time went by it became clear that, apart from God performing a miracle, she wouldn't survive outside the womb. Her spine was at 45 degrees and her vital organs were outside her body. She wouldn't be able to sustain life once the umbilical cord was cut.

When the expectation of miscarriage passed and the likelihood of their little girl going full term became the new reality, her first-time parents named her Isabelle. At that point, their prayer requests became very specific, namely, that Isabelle would survive birth so that her mom and dad could meet her while she was still alive. God answered these prayers. For three-quarters of an hour they snuggled with their little one and then placed her into the arms of Jesus.

Trials like this challenge us to think about the value of human life from God's perspective, to consider his creative purpose for each divine image-bearer. To do so, we must think deeply about the matter of life in the womb which, sadly, is often a dangerous place for unborn children with disabilities.[18] So, let's take a peek into God's art studio—the mother's womb—to gaze at the picture provided by Psalm 139:13–16:

> *For you formed my inward parts;*
> *    you knitted me together in my mother's womb.*
> *I praise you, for I am fearfully and wonderfully made.*
> *Wonderful are your works;*
> *    my soul knows it very well.*
> *My frame was not hidden from you,*
> *when I was being made in secret,*
> *    intricately woven in the depths of the earth.*
> *Your eyes saw my unformed substance;*
> *in your book were written, every one of them,*
> *    the days that were formed for me,*
> *    when as yet there was none of them.*

In this psalm, the Holy Spirit provides a "biblical ultrasound," a picture of God at work, designing a human life. In King David's reflection on the handiwork of God, we take notice of six important observations about unborn human life.

## Each Unborn Human Life Is a Unique, Well-Crafted Work of Divine Art

Life in the womb brings glory to God. *He* is the active subject: "*you* formed my inward parts; *you* knitted me together in my mother's womb" (Psalm 139:13). The womb is God's art studio, created and governed by him. It's also God's science lab, where he shapes and fashions miniature image-bearers. In addition, it's like a temple, in that everything God does there is sacred. Therefore, the human reproductive process—from conception to birth—and the life-sustaining environment of the womb must be guarded with the utmost care. Nothing must be done to harm it. It is here in the womb that God performs his most glorious creative work of crafting human beings, no two of which are exactly the same. Even parents of twins affirm that their children are not identical in every possible way. Each child is a unique creation of God, an immortal soul.

## Each Unborn Human Life, Being Crafted by God, Is Made for His Glory and Praise

As David reflects on God's careful, deliberate work in the womb, his heart and mouth pour forth praise: "I praise you, for I am fearfully and wonderfully made. Wonderful are your works; my soul knows it very well" (139:14). In Isaiah 43:7, God reveals his purpose in creating mankind: "everyone who is called by my name . . . I created for my glory, whom I formed and made." The writer of Psalm 71 agrees:

> For you, O Lord, are my hope,
>     my trust, O LORD, from my youth.
> Upon you I have leaned from before my birth;
>     you are he who took me from my mother's
>     womb.
> My praise is continually of you.
>
> (Psalm 71:5–6)

The good purposes of God guide him along as he uniquely crafts each human life. The end result is that, even though we may not be able to see or comprehend his ways in this life, God is always up to something good. When we come to this realization, we, too, will give him glory, honor, and praise.

## Each Unborn Human Life, Though Not Fully Visible to the Human Eye, Is under the Watchful Eye of God

Since the 1500s, Swiss watchmakers have built a reputation for being the finest engineers of timekeeping instruments in the world. Yet they are no match for the Creator of the human body. While a baby is in the womb, God carefully assembles 300–350 miniature bones into a little girl or boy. After birth, this baby typically grows into adulthood. In order for the baby to be able to pass through the birth canal, over one hundred of these bones were once flexible, but now fuse together to make the 206 bones of the adult frame. No wonder David sings to God, "My frame was not hidden from you, when I was being made in secret, intricately woven in the depths of the earth. Your eyes saw my unformed substance" (139:15–16).

This work, David says, is done "in secret," unbeknownst even to the baby's mother. By the time the average woman recognizes she is pregnant, the baby's fingers and toes are beginning to appear as buds. The arms can already flex at the elbows and wrists, the eyes have begun to develop pigment, and the intestines are getting longer. Though all of this is unknown to the mother, God is very attentive. Here in this dark, safe place called the *womb* God does his creative work in secret, typically making the parents wait nine months before unveiling his masterpiece.

## Each Unborn Human Life Is Designed to Fit into God's Grand Design for Mankind and for the World

God's intimate care for David while yet in his mother's womb gave him great confidence that nothing he went through in this life could somehow slip by God unnoticed. "And in Your book," he writes, "were all written the days that were ordained for me, when as yet there was not one of them" (139:16 NASB).

In the midst of his great suffering, the Old Testament patriarch Job was also comforted by this fundamental truth:

*Remember that you have made me like clay;*
*and will you return me to the dust?*
*Did you not pour me out like milk*
*and curdle me like cheese?*
*You clothed me with skin and flesh,*
*and knit me together with bones and sinews.*
*You have granted me life and steadfast love,*
*and your care has preserved my spirit.*

(Job 10:9–12)

This truth was very comforting to my wife and me as we contemplated our granddaughter's brief life. Every human life is of immeasurable value regardless of abilities or disabilities, or how long the person lives. Since every human's life is created in the image of God, and his or her definite purpose is ordained by God, every human life should be protected from harm and treated with utmost dignity. Some may be tempted to think of our granddaughter's very brief life as a failed pregnancy, but it was nothing of the sort. Isabelle's days were ordained for her, and, even in a very short time, she did more to impact people for the gospel and the glory of God than we may ever know.

## Each Unborn Human Life Possesses Untold Potential to Declare: "God, You Are Worthy of Praise"

Even the cry of an infant is a tribute to God. Though sometimes annoying to us, it's music to the Creator's ears. Let's be honest: too often we are guilty of treating children like inconveniences or interruptions to our own plans. Sadly, we are even sometimes like Jesus' disciples who just wanted the annoying kids to go away. But Jesus gently rebuked them, saying, "Let the children come to me, and do not hinder them, for to such belongs the kingdom of God" (Luke 18:16). Children often bring pure and beautiful praise to God, because they possess the simplicity of faith which we often lose as we get older.

Religious pride leads us to think we understand more than children do and, therefore, are of more value. But we are wrong, as were the religious leaders on that first Palm Sunday:

> *But when the chief priests and the scribes saw*
> *the wonderful things that He had done, and the*
> *children who were shouting in the temple, "Hosanna*
> *to the Son of David," they became indignant and*
> *said to Him, "Do You hear what these children are*
> *saying?" And Jesus said to them, "Yes; have you*
> *never read, 'Out of the mouth of infants and nursing*
> *babies You have prepared praise for Yourself'?"*
>
> (Matthew 21:15–16 NASB)

In the minds of the religious leaders, children should be seen and not heard. Yet God's Word makes it clear that there is nothing so pleasant to the Creator's ears than the praise that flows from the lips of children.

Therefore, David says, "I praise you, for I am fearfully and wonderfully made. Wonderful are your works; my soul knows it very well" (Psalm 139:14). David came to the realization that each and every unborn human life has untold potential to declare praise to his or her Creator.

## Each Unborn Human Life Is Not Alone in the Womb: God Is with Each Little Girl or Boy

This truth is implied by the context of Psalm 139. David, the songwriter, is now an adult who is reflecting upon God's faithful care for him throughout his life, beginning in the womb. "Where shall I go from your Spirit? Or where shall I flee from your presence?" he asks God (139:7). These are rhetorical questions, of course. The answer is already known. David can't go anywhere without God also being there. Even down unknown paths "your hand shall lead me," and when I am weak "your right hand shall hold me" (139:10).

These assurances stemmed from knowing that God was present every moment of every day *while* he was in his mother's womb: "For you formed my inward parts; you knitted me together in my mother's womb" (139:13). What a beautiful picture! Though we may wonder what the divine Artist is up to, especially when birth defects and disabilities are discovered while the baby is developing in the womb, we can be confident that God's good and perfect will for each life is being carried out.

Trusting God in the winding journey of life means holding on tightly to simple truths we can count on, no matter how circumstances may change. Of course there are questions we will never be able to answer, especially when disability enters the picture, but this one fact we do know: our God is the all-wise and good Creator whose purpose and counsel far exceed ours. When God knit each of our ten little ones in my wife's womb, the Lord utilized a genetic weakness in both of us to determine that some of our children would be hearing impaired. In addition, he directed other mysterious "defects" to cluster in Kayte's prenatal development to create a uniquely precious girl. According to Psalm 139, our God—her God—fashioned her in certain ways because he already had her days fashioned in his mind.

*From Joni's Heart . . .*

As a painter, I'm a little hesitant to invite observers into my art studio while I am rendering a work. Once, while I was painting a landscape, a friend wandered up behind me to watch. For many long moments, he quietly observed my brush strokes as I worked. Occasionally he whispered encouraging comments, and I could tell he was delighted to see my painting begin to take shape before his eyes.

After some time, I leaned back to admire the half-finished rendering of a cabin on the side of a hill, with faraway mountains brooding in the distance. Sunrays bursting through clouds gave the piece of art an airy, light feeling. After a minute or two, I dabbed my brush into a dark, moody gray and made two or three strong vertical strokes that obscured the lovely background. From behind me, I heard, "What! Why did you do that? Are you trying to ruin your own painting?"

I could understand his dismay. To all appearances, it looked like I had intentionally ruined an otherwise pleasant picture—the strong, dark vertical lines did not seem to fit into the overall composition. Things were going well, the painting was taking on a sensible shape, and then . . . bam! What was this? A terrible mistake on the part of me, the artist? Had I suffered a mental relapse? Was I displeased with the painting, and so became thoughtless and reckless with my brush? Had I stopped caring about my work?

Not at all.

All along, those "ugly" marks on the picture were part of my original design. From the very beginning, I intended that they should be part of the composition. My friend standing behind me, however, had no idea—he couldn't read my mind, and so was not privy to my intent. Not understanding the way compositions evolve, he second-guessed me. But I went ahead and worked on, smearing my brush into later shades of green mixed with gray. As I continued working, soon my intention became clear: the three strong vertical strokes had become trunks of pine trees. And as I applied lighter tones of green and brown, branches began to emerge, and then twigs and boughs of fluffy pine needles.

All along, I had wanted to frame the brightly lit cabin scene with a dark canopy of pine trees. It gave the painting a greater depth of field and focused the eye on the little cabin nestled snugly among the trees with mountains in the distance. The painting would have been lacking, incomplete, without those trees—which all started with three ugly "mistakes," or, rather, three strong vertical brushstrokes.

My friend forgot all about my so-called error when he stood back and took in the final rendering. "I can't remember what it was like before," he commented. "You've done a beautiful thing."

Parents often say the same to me after years of raising a child with a disability. As God's purposes unfold, their sobering ideas about disability begin to soften, and blessings out of brokenness are revealed.

So, the painting of a cabin framed by trees is a fitting metaphor for Psalm 139:13, 15–16 (NIV):

*For you created my inmost being;*
*you knit me together in my mother's womb. . . .*
*My frame was not hidden from you*
*when I was made in the secret place,*
*when I was woven together in the depths of the earth.*
*Your eyes saw my unformed body;*
*all the days ordained for me were written in*
*your book*
*before one of them came to be.*

Too often, we are like my friend who walked up behind me in my art studio. We watch the way God works in our lives and, after some time, think we have a fairly clear idea of where he's taking us. But like my friend, we are not privy to God's intentions and design as the Artist. Plus, we are clueless as to God's ways with those unexpected "dark marks." When suddenly the picture of our life takes a somber, unexpected turn—the birth of a child with multiple disabilities or a life-altering accident—we immediately assume God has made a terrible mistake. He has become careless and unthinking. He has stopped caring about "the work of his hands" in our lives.

Not so. "The LORD will fulfill his purpose for me," says Psalm 138:8. Not only will God fulfill his purpose for you and your spouse, he will also fulfill his glorious purpose for your child.

Yes, he will do a beautiful thing.

*Joni*

# Chapter 5

# Dependent by Design, Disabled on Purpose

*But we have this treasure in jars of clay, to show
that the surpassing power belongs to God and
not to us. We are afflicted in every way, but not
crushed; perplexed, but not driven to despair;
persecuted, but not forsaken; struck down, but
not destroyed; always carrying in the body the
death of Jesus, so that the life of Jesus may also be
manifested in our bodies.*

(2 Corinthians 4:7–10)

God's ways often present a paradox. He is often glorified more
when we are subjected to forms of suffering that the world
thinks make us less valuable or useful than others. In and through
our weakness God's power is made more evident, not only to us
who must rely upon it day by day, but also to those who observe
us. As a result, God is praised for his works.

In *A Lifetime of Wisdom*, Joni Eareckson Tada shares a story
that beautifully illustrates this truth:

> It was Talent Night at one of our Joni and Friends
> family retreats and Cindy, a young woman with
> severe cerebral palsy, was the last one scheduled to
> perform. Cindy's mother pushed her daughter in the
> wheelchair out onto the platform. Cindy, she told us,
> had been working hard all week on her song "Amazing
> Grace." Several of us looked at each other. We all loved

*Cindy, but how was this going to work? Because of her disability, Cindy couldn't speak. Then her mother walked off stage and left Cindy alone. The young woman laboriously stretched out her twisted fingers and pushed a button on her communication device attached to her chair and out came the monotone computerized voice, "Amazing grace, how sweet the sound, that saved a wretch like me." As the robotic voice continued the hymn, Cindy turned her head to face us, the audience, and with enormous effort began to mouth all the words as best she could. What's more, her smile lit up the entire place. It was a performance that any opera star or recording artist would envy. To be honest, I've never seen anything equal to it. "Amazing Grace" is not a new song, but that night it was sung in an entirely new way. Although Cindy was unable to sing the words with her vocal cords, something happened as she leaned hard on Jesus and mouthed those words. I can't explain how, but somehow it rose up in that auditorium as a ringing hymn of praise to God. It was as though Cindy's song was backed by an 80-piece orchestra. I can imagine angels leaning over the edge of heaven, filled with wonder, to catch every word.*[19]

This is the main point in the Scripture at the beginning of this chapter. The apostle Paul gives us a roadmap to thinking biblically about the paradoxical importance of weakness and disability.

## God Displays His Power through Weakness

When the apostle declares, "But we have this treasure in jars of clay," the treasure he has in mind is the gospel (2 Corinthians 4:7). We know this because of the preceding verses, which speak of how the gospel is veiled to unbelievers, because Satan has blinded their minds so that they do not see the glory of Jesus Christ

(4:3–4). But "God, who said, 'Let light shine out of darkness,' has shone in our hearts to give the light of the knowledge of the glory of God in the face of Jesus Christ" (4:6).

The treasure believers possess is "the light of the knowledge of the glory of God in the face of Jesus Christ," that is, the gospel. It is the good news that "Christ Jesus came into the world to save sinners" (1 Timothy 1:15). This saving knowledge of Jesus is invaluable. We do not possess this treasure because we are worthy, but as the result of the supernatural work of the Holy Spirit applying the gospel to our hearts. Since the gospel is a treasure, the greatest treasure of all is the Christ of whom the gospel speaks. But where does this treasure reside? Where is it housed? This priceless treasure is put on display in the lives of those who are weak.

## God's Chosen Container Is Fragile

The container God selected for the gospel is the fragile human body: "But we have this treasure in jars of clay." We know Paul is referring to the body, since he speaks of always carrying about in the body—that is, our mortal flesh—the dying of Jesus (2 Corinthians 4:10–11). Jars of clay, common pottery in Paul's day, are described in this way by *The MacArthur Study Bible*:

> *They were cheap, breakable, and replaceable but they served necessary household functions. Sometimes they were used as a vault to store valuables, such as money, jewelry, or important documents. But they were most often used for holding garbage and human waste. The latter is the use Paul had in mind, and it was how Paul viewed himself, as lowly, common, expendable, and replaceable (cf. 1 Cor. 1:20–27; 2 Tim. 2:20, 21).[20]*

The grace of God is exhibited more powerfully when it flows from a weak life; it is displayed as more valuable when it energizes the weak person. This is contrary to how we typically think.

69

Perhaps you think that power comes from strength, not weakness, and, consequently, it makes you uncomfortable to think that it may be better for your mind and body to be weak than to be strong. But God accomplishes more through us, for his glory, when we are increasingly dependent upon him. This doesn't make sense from a human perspective—it makes no sense at all. But God often turns man's wisdom on its head.

## Weakness Draws Attention to God's Sufficiency

The reason God houses the priceless treasure of the gospel within the weakness of human flesh is to draw attention to the sufficiency of his power, not ours: "to show that the surpassing power belongs to God and not to us" (2 Corinthians 4:7). God does this intentionally; it's not an accident. God places the infinite value of knowing Jesus inside fragile jars of clay, in order to make his presence more obvious. "Such is the confidence that we have through Christ toward God" (3:4). What confidence, Paul? "Not that we are sufficient in ourselves to claim anything as coming from us, but our sufficiency is from God, who has made us sufficient to be ministers of a new covenant, not of the letter but of the Spirit. For the letter kills, but the Spirit gives life" (3:5–6). The answer to a lack of confidence in ourselves is not to boost our self-confidence, but to understand that we are inadequate and weak. However, if you are a Christian, you possess a sufficiency that is not from yourself but from Christ. It is, therefore, supernatural. Your sufficiency is "from God."

God houses the priceless treasure of the gospel within the weakness of human flesh because he wants the world to see his strength. One way to do that is to cause us to be weak, so that he might show himself as strong. This is even the case in calling us to salvation. According to Scripture, we are called to faith in Christ, not because we are strong and have so much potential to offer to God, but rather because we are weak, because we are fragile. God rarely chooses the wise or strong for salvation (1 Corinthians 1:26–29).

## Physical Weakness Highlights Life in Jesus

Physical suffering is a foretaste of death which draws attention to the only true source of life: Jesus. To make his point, Paul uses four descriptions of the suffering that he and his coworkers experienced. "We are afflicted in every way," he says, "but not crushed" (2 Corinthians 4:8). The word "afflicted" means "tightly squeezed" and refers to being under intense pressure and burdened in spirit. We are subject to pressure, but we are not crushed or trapped in a confined, narrow space. Like Paul, we may also be "perplexed," that is, at a loss or in doubt, but we won't be despondent to the final point of despair. Then, we are persecuted, but not forsaken (4:9). The word "persecuted" means to be hunted down like an animal. Sometimes we feel as if we are living prey, but we are not forsaken, deserted, or abandoned. The word "forsaken" means to be abandoned by someone in our time of difficulty. Remember that even if you feel forgotten by everyone, the Lord will never abandon you. Jesus said, "I will never leave you nor forsake you" (Hebrews 13:5). Finally, we may be struck down, but we won't be destroyed. "Struck down" means thrown down, as in a wrestling match. Numerous times this happened to the apostle. He was beaten, left for dead, and struck down. But he was not destroyed; he did not perish.

Yes, we may be thrown down by the trials of life; however, if we know the Lord, we will never be destroyed. Paul knew he would not perish one minute earlier than God had destined for him to perish. His life was in God's hands.

*For we do not want you to be unaware, brothers,*
*of the affliction we experienced in Asia. For we*
*were so utterly burdened beyond our strength that*
*we despaired of life itself. Indeed, we felt that we*
*had received the sentence of death. But that was*
*to make us rely not on ourselves but on God who*
*raises the dead. He delivered us from such a deadly*
*peril, and he will deliver us. On him we have set*
*our hope that he will deliver us again.*

(2 Corinthians 1:8–10)

71

Why did God ordain this kind of suffering for Paul and his companions? The apostle gives a surprising answer: so that they would not trust in themselves but in "God who raises the dead" (1:9). God ordains weakness and suffering so that we will not trust in ourselves, but in him alone.

Suffering might feel like death, but in God's economy it actually produces life. Paul described himself as "always carrying in the body the death of Jesus" (2 Corinthians 4:10). This was always the case for Paul. So, essentially, he says, "We are always thrown down and beat up by the enemy, so that the glorious, sufficient, and infinitely more valuable treasure—life in Christ—is made manifest to a watching world."

God gives greater grace to those who suffer; he gives grace to those who need it the most. "For we who live are always being given over to death for Jesus' sake, so that the life of Jesus also may be manifested in our mortal flesh" (4:11). He's saying the same thing he did in 4:10, just in a different way. We're constantly being delivered over. We're constantly being handed over like the criminal who is about to be hanged. In our weakness, we slowly walk to the executioner's stand, so that the life of Jesus may be manifested in our mortal flesh. Physical weakness is a form of death which draws attention to the only source of true life: Jesus.

## Dying to Self Leads to Spiritual Life in Others

Deathlike suffering might afflict us, but while we are being afflicted, we are also being strengthened by the grace of God. "Death works in us," Paul says, but life works in others. In John 12:24, Jesus announced that the hour of his death—the hour in which he would be glorified—was coming soon: "Truly, truly, I say to you, unless a grain of wheat falls into the earth and dies, it remains alone; but if it dies, it bears much fruit." Of course, Jesus was speaking prophetically about his death on the cross. The seed of his life would go into the ground, so to speak, and grow into a harvest. This harvest is called the church; it is all those who receive eternal life as the result of his death.

God's power is beautifully demonstrated through human weakness, and God's plan to exalt the infinite value of knowing Christ requires death. Death to self. Death to personal dreams and agendas. Death to what we thought our life would be like. God's grace overcomes our weakness, as he delights to demonstrate his power through our fragile vessel. May each of us be fully surrendered to our Lord, so that he will truly be free to use our weaknesses in any way he desires!

## Weakness Is a Platform for Greater Grace

It's common for some Christians to say to others who suffer, "Rest assured, God will not give you more than you can handle." But I often wonder what they really mean and whether it's true. If what they mean is that God's love toward us is so protective that he will never give us more than *we* can bear, then the statement is false. But if what is meant is that in the midst of indescribable suffering which brings us to our weakest point, God empowers and equips us so thoroughly in the inner person that we are able to bear up under it—with *his* strength—then the statement is true. I do not believe that God gives us only what we can handle. Instead, he intentionally gives us what we cannot handle, in and of ourselves, so that we are driven to depend upon him and the all-sufficient resources that belong to us in Christ. If God gave us only what we could handle, where would the glory be? Who would get the credit? Instead, God receives greater glory when we humbly receive the gift of suffering, since it systematically breaks down more and more of Self, so that Christ may be all in all. A prime example of this principle is seen in the life of the apostle Paul, who writes,

> *Three times I pleaded with the Lord about this ["thorn in the flesh"], that it should leave me. But he said to me, "My grace is sufficient for you, for my power is made perfect in weakness." Therefore I will boast all the more gladly of my weaknesses, so that the power of Christ may rest upon me. For the*

*sake of Christ, then, I am content with weaknesses,
insults, hardships, persecutions, and calamities.
For when I am weak, then I am strong.*

(2 Corinthians 12:8–10)

In this chapter the apostle is describing a revelation that he received from God, and what Jesus said about its purpose in his life. Read the verses above again.

In the previous verses of this chapter, Paul speaks about his experience in the third person, as if he is not the man he is describing. He does this because he's reluctant to tell others. In fact, he's been silent for fourteen years. But because his accusers have pushed him to the wall, he no longer has a choice. For the sake of the integrity of the gospel and his ministry, he must now disclose his experience.

The enemies in Corinth were "super apostles" who claimed they were better than Paul, who was an inferior man in their eyes. They had already criticized him for being an unpolished speaker (2 Corinthians 11:6), so this would only have given them one more thing to ridicule. That is why he says "Boasting is necessary" (12:1 NASB). Now it was necessary for him to open up about this revelation, because the welfare of the gospel ministry was at stake. Paul says he was taken up to the *third heaven,* which is the dwelling place of God.

Scripture describes three heavens. The first heaven is the sky and the atmosphere that most closely surrounds us, the air we breathe. The second heaven is the travel space for the planets and the solar system. Yet there is a third heaven that is beyond all that we can see. Like Jesus, Paul calls it p*aradise.* To the repentant thief on the cross who looked to Jesus with the eyes of simple faith, the Savior said, "Today you will be with me in paradise" (Luke 23:43).

When he was caught up to the very dwelling place of God, Paul saw and heard things that were beyond being inexpressible, but was commanded not to talk about them. Paul's great revelation was then followed by a particular affliction: "So to keep me from becoming conceited because of the surpassing greatness of the revelations, a thorn was given me in the flesh, a messenger of Satan to harass me, to keep me from becoming conceited. Three times I pleaded with the Lord about this . . ." (2 Corinthians 12:7–8). In these verses, Paul now shifts to the first-person pronoun, revealing that he indeed is this man. Because of the surpassing greatness of the revelations, Paul would have been tempted to exalt himself. Therefore, God gave him a thorn in the flesh, a messenger of Satan to torment him.

What was this affliction? He describes it as a "thorn" (*scolops* in the Greek, referring to a long, sharp stake). Whatever it was, it felt as if a pointed stake was being driven through him. It seems best to understand this as some kind of physical weakness that regularly beat him up.

Paul's response to his thorn in the flesh was passionate prayer. Three times he begged the Lord to take this affliction away, but God refused. Instead of removing the thorn, Jesus said to Paul, "My grace is sufficient for you, for my power is made perfect in weakness" (12:9). That is shorthand for "No, Paul, I will not take it away from you." Paul was brought to a necessary place of submission to the will of God. In this way, Paul was becoming conformed to the likeness of Jesus, who cried out three times in the garden of Gethsemane, "Father, if you are willing, remove this cup from me. Nevertheless, not my will, but yours, be done" (Luke 22:42). Each time the Lord Jesus surrendered his will to the Father's good plan. Three times Paul cried out to God, "Remove this from me." But God said, "No, I won't remove it," so he didn't ask a fourth time.

Paul recognized that even though his physical disability came through Satan, it was ultimately from God. Satan was the agency through whom the problem came, but he was the secondary cause. He was merely the delivery boy, the messenger used to deliver the "package of suffering" to Paul; he was not the ultimate source. God was the "principal cause," as he was in the book of Job. Satan most certainly thought the affliction would drive the apostle away from the Lord, perhaps in anger, resentment, and bitterness. But he was wrong. Instead, it propelled Paul to an even closer walk with God.

## Benefits of Paul's Affliction

What were God's reasons for bringing this thorn of suffering into Paul's life? The apostle reveals three benefits that he experienced.

### Suffering Prevents Conceit

First, God gave the apostle his affliction in order to cultivate an increase in humility: "So to *keep me from becoming conceited* because of the surpassing greatness of the revelations, a thorn was given me." The revelations Paul received were so great that the uniqueness of his experience was sure to produce an arrogance that would hinder his usefulness. To keep him from raising himself up, God introduced an instrument for the production of humility. Why would God do this? Because "God opposes the proud but gives grace to the humble" (James 4:6; 1 Peter 5:5). God takes no pleasure in opposing his servants, but he will do so if it is necessary.

Physical disability was given to the apostle to prevent pride from taking a deeper hold of his heart, resulting in a more limited usefulness to God. God had prepared a large, broad ministry for Paul, and his thorn in the flesh was given to prepare him to glorify God in that ministry.

### Suffering Portrays the Sufficiency of God's Empowering Grace

Second, God gave Paul his physical trial to demonstrate the power of grace: "he said to me, 'My grace is sufficient for you'" (12:9). God's grace and kindness would continue to be enough to help him endure his physical weakness so that God could continue to use him for his purposes. Paul wrote of this empowering grace in his first letter to the church at Corinth: "But by the grace of God I am what I am, and his grace toward me was not in vain [futile, useless]. On the contrary, I worked harder than any of them, though it was not I, but the grace of God that is with me" (1 Corinthians 15:10).

Paul understood that God's grace not only saved him from the eternal punishment of his sin, but also empowered him for the Christian life and ministry. Each time Paul came to the point where he thought he couldn't go on, God's grace energized him. Through Paul's affliction, God painted a portrait of his sufficiency. This means that if Paul had not been given this affliction, undue attention would have been drawn to the apostle instead of to the God whom he served.

## Suffering Perfects the Power of Christ

The third reason God gave the apostle his affliction was to perfect the power of Christ within him. The term "made perfect" means to fulfill or bring to completion. "My power is made perfect in weakness" means that the power of Christ is fulfilled, or brought to its intended end, through weakness, not strength. God designed it this way.

The contrast of our weakness with God's power brings God the glory he deserves. Without Paul's thorn in the flesh, the glory of Christ would have been minimized in Paul's life. That's the opposite of how we naturally think. We think physical or intellectual disabilities equal limitations. Not a chance in God's program! Instead they actually lead to greater glory, because the vessel appears inadequate. Thus God receives more glory.

Disability is a larger platform for greater grace. That is at least partly what God has in mind for you. If your child, spouse, or other family member has disabilities, then his or her suffering and your daily weakness become a platform for the display of greater grace. If you are the one with a disability, then God's grace is sufficient for you, too. From God's perspective, the only limitations that exist are the ones we create. This is why the apostle could so boldly proclaim: "Therefore I will boast all the more gladly of my weaknesses, so that the power of Christ may rest upon me. For the sake of Christ, then, I am content with weaknesses, insults, hardships, persecutions, and calamities. For when I am weak, then I am strong" (12:9–10).

*From Joni's Heart . . .*

In our society, we avoid suffering—running away from it if we can, or numbing its effects if we can't. Even Christ-followers struggle with this. At the onset of a life-transforming injury or the birth of a child with disabilities, our faith is shaken to the core. Instinctively, we want the comfortable and convenient way. Unless our hearts are firmly anchored in God's promises, or our faith has been proven and refined through earlier disappointments, we will easily collapse under life-altering troubles that foretell doom and gloom.

In the early years of my quadriplegia I was horrified at the prospect of remaining paralyzed for the rest of my life. But once my heart became riveted to God's promises, once my faith survived the initial refining, God's design began to dawn. It was clear: heaven and hell had participated in my terrible accident, but for different reasons.

Perhaps hell hoped to shipwreck my faith, but heaven helped me take every thought captive to the obedience of Christ, especially when my thoughts tended toward resentment. My paralysis pushed me into times of prayer, often when I did not *want* to pray. I became more patient with people, humbly admitting when I was demanding and unappreciative (I've got a long way to go before I'm entirely sanctified!). My wheelchair helped me to enlarge my eternal estate: my disability kept forcing me to choose things that increased my capacity for joy in heaven, not things that diminished it.

I was able to tell my friends, "God's refusal to make my life easier has been my greatest blessing." I became convinced that deep faith, strong character, heartfelt compassion, and a greater dependence on Christ were the *best* of blessings. I had the assurance that although my disability itself was grueling, the result would be God's best for my life. Even a broken neck can be God's plan A. How so? Let me explain with this little story.

My signature earrings are hammered gold, with crinkled edges that almost sparkle. They were once smooth polished squares, an unexpected gift from a dear friend after I admired them. I wore them constantly, but one day at work, one of the precious earrings slipped off my ear. As I wheeled to get help, I heard a sickening crunch: my treasured earring was impaled on my wheelchair tire.

I took the crushed earring to a local jeweler, who said it couldn't be fixed; the damage was too great. He did, however, offer to alter the smooth one to match the other. I was hesitant to potentially ruin this beautiful set of gold earrings, but I decided to trust him. After all, he was the jeweler. He was the expert, and I wasn't.

As I waited, I heard pounding and grinding from the back and wondered if the jeweler knew what he was doing. Soon he returned with a matching second gold earring. It was horribly marred and mangled, but strangely magnificent, resembling the work of a skilled artist. The hammering had produced something breathtakingly beautiful. Plus, the new set of earrings, crunched and crinkled, reflected the light more brilliantly—they were plan A earrings, not plan B or C. And the earrings became a metaphor for my life.

This is a fitting metaphor for your life, too, as you discover a deeper devotion to Jesus Christ through this season of hardship. God knows what he's doing as he hammers, shapes, and bends us so that we can better reflect his glory. After all, God is the Master Jeweler, and we are not. He is the expert, and we'd do well to yield to him. He's got a great plan A design in mind!

*When God wants to drill a man,*
*And thrill a man,*
*And skill a man*
*When God wants to mold a man*
*To play the noblest part;*

*When He yearns with all His heart*
*To create so great and bold a man*
*That all the world shall be amazed,*
*Watch His methods, watch His ways!*

*How He ruthlessly perfects*
*Whom He royally elects!*
*How He hammers him and hurts him,*
*And with mighty blows converts him*

*Into trial shapes of clay which*
*Only God understands;*
*While his tortured heart is crying*
*And he lifts beseeching hands!*

*How He bends but never breaks*
*When His good He undertakes;*
*How He uses whom He chooses,*
*And with every purpose fuses him;*
*By every act induces him*
*To try His splendor out—*
*God knows what He's about.*[21]

*Joni*

# Chapter 6

# Doing Life Together in Gracious Community

*On the contrary, the parts of the body that seem to be weaker are indispensable.*

(1 Corinthians 12:22)

In church life, it's not enough to do various activities together. We need to do them together as a community, a family, as we learn to follow Christ and love one another. If we simply gather to attend "the main event," without cultivating an atmosphere that breathes grace, acceptance, and full involvement, then we are merely a religious organization. But the local church is much more than that: it's a functioning body.

*For just as the body is one and has many members, and all the members of the body, though many, are one body, so it is with Christ. For in one Spirit we were all baptized into one body—Jews or Greeks, slaves or free—and all were made to drink of one Spirit.*

*For the body does not consist of one member but of many. If the foot should say, "Because I am not a hand, I do not belong to the body," that would not make it any less a part of the body. And if the ear should say, "Because I am not an eye, I do not belong to the body," that would not make it any less a part of the body. If the whole body were an eye, where would be the sense of hearing? If the whole body were an ear, where would be the sense*

> *of smell? But as it is, God arranged the members in the body, each one of them, as he chose. If all were a single member, where would the body be? As it is, there are many parts, yet one body.*
>
> *The eye cannot say to the hand, "I have no need of you," nor again the head to the feet, "I have no need of you." On the contrary, the parts of the body that seem to be weaker are indispensable, and on those parts of the body that we think less honorable we bestow the greater honor, and our unpresentable parts are treated with greater modesty, which our more presentable parts do not require. But God has so composed the body, giving greater honor to the part that lacked it, that there may be no division in the body, but that the members may have the same care for one another. If one member suffers, all suffer together; if one member is honored, all rejoice together.*
>
> (1 Corinthians 12:12–26)

According to God's design the church is a living organism, energized and sustained by the life of the Holy Spirit. Together we worship God, spread the gospel, and build up one another in submission to the headship of Jesus Christ. That's essentially what the Scripture above teaches us.

The church is not merely *like* a body, it *is* a body. It's a living body made up of many parts, every one of which is indispensable to the overarching purpose of God. Therefore, the apostle places the human body before our minds as a visual of the sometimes-hidden work of God. My aim in this chapter is to help you to see how beautifully God has designed his body, the church, to function so that it draws attention to the grace of the gospel. More specifically, I want to help you to appreciate how God uses disability to magnify his grace by employing it to complete the church. The teaching of the apostle opens a window to three ways God wants us to respond to his brilliant design.

## Appreciate the Oneness of God's Design

Notice how many times the apostle uses the word "one" in these two sentences: "For just as the body is *one* and has many members, and all the members of the body, though many, are *one* body, so it is with Christ. For in *one* Spirit we were all baptized into *one* body . . . the body does not consist of *one* member but of many" (1 Corinthians 12:12–14).

God created the human body as an incredible machine, a multitude of different parts working together to form one person. The 206 bones in our body are composed of 300 pieces. This skeletal framework, along with 650 muscles that weave in and around it, holds in place seventy-eight organs and twelve major systems. If that's not enough to boggle our minds, consider that within these parts there are approximately 37.6 trillion cells working together all of the time so that our bodies function properly. All of these parts cooperate with one another so effectively that we would never think to look at a person and say, "Well, there goes a bunch of parts." Instead we see a whole person, one body made up of many parts, all designed for a unified purpose. Some are weak or less important, from our human vantage point, and some are strong and appear more important. But each serves the purpose for which it was engineered by God. So it is in the body of Christ, the church. No single part is more important than another; every part is indispensable. All are designed to live and work together in gracious community. This is the Holy Spirit's design for the church: "For in one Spirit we were all baptized into one body."

The doctrine of the baptism of the Holy Spirit is quite simple. At the moment of salvation, God places us into the body of Christ. He immerses us into the church, and adopts us into his family. The Spirit of God carries out this work of the Lord in order to create his intended oneness. We have so much in common with all who believe in the Lord Jesus Christ as our Savior and the only atoning sacrifice for our sins. Recognizing the Spirit's work in our salvation leads us to appreciate the oneness of God's design.

It's been well said that "The ground is level at the foot of the cross." We all equally need the mercy of God and the gospel's saving power. Therefore, we are all in this together. As followers of Christ who are living with or without disabilities, we do life together. Our calling is to live together in gracious community. This is not by accident; it's according to God's design. Recognizing the wisdom of God's plan helps us to avoid two common errors that hinder togetherness.

## Avoid the Two Sides of Self-Focus

When God first created man and woman in his image, the world was perfect; it was free from the presence and consequences of sin. In that state, the human body was free of dysfunction, defect, or disorder. But Adam's and Eve's rejection of God's perfect order led to the fall of all mankind into sin, which had a negative impact on the physical world, including our bodies. Additionally, it had an impact upon us spiritually, which continues to hinder the proper functioning of the church. As Paul continues his teaching, he identifies two different, yet related, problematic thought patterns. Both are fueled by pride, which is essentially an inaccurate view of ourselves.

### "I Am Less Important Than Others, Because of My Weaknesses"

The first problematic thought pattern could be stated this way: "I am less gifted and, therefore, am not an important part of the church." Paul gently rebukes this error:

> If the foot should say, "Because I am not a hand,
> I do not belong to the body," that would not make
> it any less a part of the body. And if the ear should
> say, "Because I am not an eye, I do not belong to
> the body," that would not make it any less a part of
> the body.

(12:15–16)

Paul corrects this proud attitude of belittling oneself, which says, "I'm not good enough because I don't have the gifts and abilities that other people have." This subtle side of pride leads a person to conclude, "If I can't serve the church in the way I think I should be able to serve the church, then I'm not going to do anything." It's as if one of my eyes were to say, "I don't like being an eye. I'm sick of it. I've been an eye for fifty-five years. I'd rather be a foot or a bicep, so I'm going to stop being an eye." You can imagine how well that would go!

The apostle's correction comes in the form of a new attitude. In other words, if we tend to belittle ourselves, we need humility. We need to understand what it means to be *inter*dependent, not independent. In the Christian life, independence becomes a hindrance. God created us to be interdependent—that is, dependent upon one another and, of course, dependent on him. The humility of interdependence says, "I may not have that other person's gifts and abilities. Nonetheless, I'm a necessary part of the body. God uniquely gifted and equipped me to be a blessing to my church. It may not be in a prominent way, but it will be just as important, since every part is indispensable."

Rather than "checking out" of church life because you are not what you want to be, the proper attitude of interdependence says, "I am who God made me to be, and therefore I want to serve him in whatever way he will allow." This leads to a humble response, such as, "I will pursue the fulfillment of my purpose in the body of Christ with contentment and joy." The Scripture continues, "But as it is, God arranged the members in the body, each one of them, as he chose" (12:18). If all were a single member, where would the body be? If every member was an eye, where would the body be? The answer is: there would be no body.

## "I Am More Important Than Others, Because of My Strengths"

The second problematic thought pattern could be stated this way: "I am more gifted than others, therefore I am a more important part of the church." This is the other side of pride. One side of pride belittles oneself, while the other exalts oneself. The apostle corrects this attitude by repeating the overarching principal: "there are many parts, yet one body" (12:20). God designed oneness into the body. He designed many different parts, yes, but to function not as many individual parts acting as they freely choose, but as one body, every part working in coordination with the others to accomplish the work of God. Just as Paul offers gentle rebuke to those who think of themselves as inferior, so he corrects those who think of themselves as superior: "The eye cannot say to the hand, 'I have no need of you,' nor again the head to the feet, 'I have no need of you'" (12:21). If the eye does not think it needs the hand, who will put your glasses on in the morning? If the eye does not need the hand, who will get the piece of sawdust out of your eye? There's no mutual benefit. On the contrary, "the parts of the body that seem to be weaker are indispensable" (12:22).

What would happen if the invisible organs stopped functioning? The whole body would be affected. It's not just the outward, showy parts of the body that are important: all are. Therefore, Paul rebukes the pride of self-sufficiency, which basically says, "Well, without me this place would fall apart." An attitude of superiority stems from believing you are irreplaceable, that God simply can't continue his work without you. Yes, you are important, but this response takes your importance too far. So the proud response that the apostle rebukes is this: "Since I am so important, I don't need others. I can function well enough without them."

If we are honest, we all have to admit that there is a little bit of these attitudes in each of us, at least once in a while. But the truth is that we desperately need each other. Paul gently corrects our misunderstanding by reminding us that every part of the body is indispensable: "on those parts of the body that we think less honorable we bestow the greater honor, and our unpresentable parts are treated with greater modesty, which our more presentable parts do not require. But God [the one in charge of the design] has so composed the body, giving greater honor to the part that lacked it" (12:23–24). The humble attitude that is needed here is the same one called for earlier: *inter*dependence. We need each other. To glorify God and make the gospel more visible, the weak need the strong and the strong need the weak. Therefore, the humble response is this: "I need the other members of the body just as much as they need me."

Imagine how much ministry could naturally occur in the life of the church if an attitude of interdependence prevailed. The mutual one-another ministry of caring would happen organically, as the outworking of our love for God and others. We wouldn't have to program a time and place for this to happen. Not that there's anything wrong with organizing events, but what our churches need more than anything is to function as living organisms. This requires humility, which leads to the preservation of unity in the body: "that there may be no division in the body, but that the members may have the same care for one another" (12:25). When we see ourselves rightly—as God sees us—engineered by him and placed into the body of Christ according to his will, we find contentment and joy by serving according to God's calling. Instead of competing against each other, or thinking we are worthless because we don't have the same giftedness, we will value one another as people who are uniquely created by God for his purpose.

Giving greater honor to the part that is lacking honor reflects that we all have the same goal, namely, to care for one another. Both self-deprecation and self-exaltation are sinful attitudes. Both are inappropriate in light of how God has designed the body of Christ. Both focus on self, not on others. Both grow out of a heart of pride, which hinders family unity. However, through the Spirit's gifting, God has already produced unity in the church that mimics the design of the human body. It's our responsibility to guard that unity, so that the body may function properly. Living together in gracious community means we need to avoid self-focus in every form.

## Adopt the Attitude of Living in Gracious Community

Appreciating the oneness of God's design should produce genuine humility, which avoids the two sides of self-focus and leads to adopting an attitude of living in gracious community. This sense of oneness also kindles empathy for one another: "If one member suffers, all suffer together; if one member is honored, all rejoice together" (12:26). Believers are not a bunch of parts randomly put together into the same organization. Nor is the church a warehouse of different parts being stored up for future use. Together we are a living organism. Therefore, when one part of the body hurts, we all hurt. If, for example, while walking through the house you happen to kick your toe against something, your whole body immediately goes to work to care for the hurting toe. Or if you strike your thumb with a hammer, every part of your body (even your vocal cords!) will jump into action to bring relief to that thumb. So it should be in the church.

Scripture exhorts: "Rejoice with those who rejoice, weep with those who weep" (Romans 12:15). Biblical compassion is not only empathetic toward those who struggle, but also others-focused enough to rejoice when God does good things for them. Let me share one personal example from twenty-nine years ago.

My wife and I were bringing our oldest son home from a visit to his audiologist. But this wasn't a typical visit. It was when he received his very first pair of hearing aids. To celebrate, we decided to stop at a toy store on the way home. As we walked into the metal-roofed store, Karen and I didn't even notice the gentle sound of rain. But the sound was completely new to our son. He couldn't stop looking up at the ceiling in wonder.

Karen will never forget what happened a few days later. She saw our toddler walking around the kitchen, touching each cabinet, the dishwasher, the stove . . . until finally his face lit up: he had found the source of the *hum* he had never heard before— it was the refrigerator! This kind of rejoicing can take place more and more in the church, too, as we learn to practice biblical empathy—to rejoice and weep with others.

Since the body is one unit made up of many parts, it's impossible for the suffering of one part not to impact the whole. This is one of the important ways in which disability blesses the church. Disability helps us to remember what we too often forget. We are one body and, therefore, we need each other. When one part struggles, we need to surround that member with love and care. God intentionally designed the church to include the parts that "seem to be weaker." It's interesting that the apostle says it this way. In our image-driven society we are taught to view bodily perfection and performance as the ultimate strength. This trains us to view a child with learning disabilities, for example, as less important or worthy of our attention than the brainy kid in class. Yet what beauty and joy are brought into our lives through children with disabilities! The same is often true of adults. Our society sometimes sees adults with disabilities as being less important, since they are unable to contribute as much (as it may seem). But God views these matters very differently. He considers each person equally valuable because he made us in his image. He has a good purpose for our lives, and his kind providence oversees every event that contributes to its fulfillment—even the events that appear to be caused by random troubles. Bad things happen, but God mysteriously works all of it together for our good.

The design of the weak and the strong, together in one body, is testimony to the glory of God's grace. According to God's goodness he has done these things. In order for there to be authentic church growth, God will often place more and more people with disabilities into our churches to show forth his manifold glory, his power, and the sufficiency of his grace. Living together in gracious community should be our commitment and aim. Our churches are not businesses or religious organizations, but living organisms, families of God. As such, we are called to love one another with the grace and acceptance that we receive in Christ. When disability teaches us to do this we heartily say, "Thank you, Lord, for the gift of disability, which reminds us that we are all dependent by design, so that you may receive all the glory, honor, and praise."

All of this reveals an important way in which disability reminds us that, deep down, we are all the same. Regardless of physical or intellectual challenges, our sinful hearts are all equally in need of the grace of God in salvation. Then, after we become Christians, we also need to live in loving community, the community of the church. We need a sense of belonging. When we see disability through the eyes of Christ,

○ We embrace human weakness as one means of making the strength of the Savior more glorious;

○ We see disability as a means whereby Self may be further dethroned, not only in our individual hearts, but also in our local churches, as we practice the Savior's selfless love within the community of grace;

○ We see disability ministry not as a separate ministry of the church, in its own separate building, but as the normal outworking of biblical love as a local family of God;

○ We truly believe that the weak members of the body are just as important as the strong, and indispensable to the proper functioning of the church.

In Christ, there is no distinction. In Christ, "abled" and "disabled" believers stand side by side as co-heirs with Christ, seated in the heavenly places with Him (Ephesians 2:6). This realization promotes selfless love, which gives birth to compassion for the sake of the gospel.

## From Joni's Heart . . .

The Sunday before writing this, during Communion, I was sitting in the pew behind Teddy and his parents. Teddy is a teenager with autism spectrum disorder (ASD) and I watched as he mischievously eyed the plate of crackers being passed down his row. Unable to speak, he groaned with delight as the plate came nearer. Before his mother could stop him, Teddy grabbed a fistful of crackers and squished them in his hand; he guffawed and proudly held up the smashed crackers. "Teddy, no!" his mother hoarsely whispered.

A different plate was passed down my row. The people in my pew gingerly reached for their piece, mindful not to touch other crackers. It was such a contrast to what Teddy did. Such fastidious care not to "contaminate" someone else's Communion bread was, to me, symbolic of the extent to which we Christians go in order to remain separate from one another. Segregated. Isolated. Independent.

When the pastor invited us to partake, my husband Ken first lifted my piece to my mouth, then he ate his. I can't take Communion by myself. I'm a little—no, a lot—like Teddy. I can't be independent. I'm forced to depend on another

Christian to help me. I used to feel awful that I needed help, but that's changed. "Asking for help" makes me feel connected. Less isolated. Interdependent. One with others. Disability is God's way of forcing a group of Christ-followers to become "smashed crackers." Bureaucracies aren't programmed to be compassionate, but Christians are.

Take my friend David Bowie, in his big, bulky wheelchair. After he became a quadriplegic in a car accident and his wife left him, he moved into a cramped one-room apartment and learned to rely on three or four part-time attendants to get him up and put him to bed. For David, life is not easy.

David has been coming to our church for several years now, but not without great effort. He can cope with In-Home Support Services and Medicare, but when it involves getting to and from church, Paratransit is a challenge: the government-subsidized transportation service couldn't care less about picking David up on time, and there are constant regulations along with new drivers with which he must contend. Sundays after worship service often mean sitting with David in an empty parking lot waiting an hour or more for his ride. It seems my quadriplegic friend is constantly jumping through bureaucratic hoops just to survive.

Another Dave, one of our church elders, lamented to me, "Sometimes Paratransit doesn't even show up at David's apartment. Last month, he and his attendant had to take two buses then wheel the last mile to church."

But Dave felt more than sad emotions; he felt ashamed. After all, our church recently acquired an unusual gift: a van with a lift. Dave knew that the real solution was simply finding available Christians who would be willing to drive David Bowie to and from church. He started calling the men in our small congregation. He found twelve who were willing to be a part of what he called "Team Transport."

Our congregation is building itself up as the stronger members care for the weaker (1 Corinthians 12:22). After all, believers are never told to become one; we *already are* one, and are expected to act like it. Ephesians 4:16 puts it this way: "From him [Christ] the whole body, joined and held together by every supporting ligament, grows and builds itself up in love, as each part does its work" (NIV). At our church, we affect one another spiritually by what we are and do individually. Therefore, if we care anything about Christ, who is the head of the body, and other Christians, the rest of the body, we simply must move beyond our comfort zones to compassionately meet needs.

God takes no delight in Emily Post picture-perfect churches, all regulated and rule-keeping. God uses disability to force the church to become smashed crackers. Communion celebrates this sort of unity in the body. We are *one* in the body of Christ, and that means we *must* live out our interdependence and intimate connection with one another. Disability has a way of pushing strong and weak congregants together as we dismantle pride, express our needs, give help, learn gratitude, receive grace, and grow up into a bunch of smashed crackers that truly resemble the body of Christ.

*Joni*

# Conclusion

Throughout this book, we've been thinking about theological truths which form a rock-solid foundation for walking by faith in a world of uncertainty. God is magnified through our weakness as well as through the short- or long-term physical and intellectual suffering we may experience in this life.

The bodies that our souls currently inhabit are temporary; they will not live forever. Our bodies are only earthly means through which God magnifies his glory by accomplishing his purposes on earth. Therefore, we need to appreciate how God uses disability, disease, and physical and mental afflictions to wean us from this earth, and to rejoice in knowing this world is not our home. Here I want to leave you with some final encouragement.

Believers in Jesus Christ can be confident, knowing "that if the tent that is our earthly home is destroyed, we have a building from God, a house not made with hands, eternal in the heavens" (2 Corinthians 5:1). Though the body we now occupy was built by God, we have another building from God that is infinitely better: we have an eternal home in heaven.

Our current flesh and blood "cannot inherit the kingdom of God, nor does the perishable inherit the imperishable" (1 Corinthians 15:50), but one day all who know Christ will be raised to receive a new, glorified body that will live in everlasting glory with the Savior. When that glorious day comes, our perishable body will put on the imperishable, and our mortal body will put on immortality (15:53). This new, resurrected body will be the eternal house for our soul, and heaven will be our eternal home. Even now, as you finish reading this book, Jesus is preparing that place for those who trust in him for their eternal salvation.

Before he left this earth and ascended into heaven, Jesus spoke these reassuring words to his followers:

> *"Let not your hearts be troubled. Believe in God;*
> *believe also in me. In my Father's house are many*
> *rooms. If it were not so, would I have told you that I*
> *go to prepare a place for you? And if I go and prepare*
> *a place for you, I will come again and will take you*
> *to myself, that where I am you may be also. And you*
> *know the way to where I am going." Thomas said*
> *to him, "Lord, we do not know where you are going.*
> *How can we know the way?" Jesus said to him, "I am*
> *the way, and the truth, and the life. No one comes to*
> *the Father except through me. If you had known me,*
> *you would have known my Father also. From now on*
> *you do know him and have seen him."*
>
> (John 14:1–7)

Consider the simple promises found in these verses. God has a big house with many rooms, which surpasses anything we've seen or can imagine. Not only is heaven a beautiful place with gates of pearl and streets of gold, but there is no darkness there. Revelation 21:23 describes the heavenly city this way: "the city has no need of sun or moon to shine on it, for the glory of God gives it light, and its lamp is the Lamb."

When Jesus told his disciples that he was leaving them soon, Thomas asked a logical question: "If we don't know where you are going, how can we know the way there?" But Jesus essentially answered, "There is a way, and I am it. The destination is not merely a place, but an eternal relationship with a person—God." What makes heaven so heavenly is the presence of God. Jesus has gone ahead of us to prepare an eternal house. One day, he will return to bring home all those who belong to him.

Perhaps the most wonderful assurance of all is that we can know the way to get there. Jesus is the way. He is the only way to the Father. The Bible teaches that we can know that we are saved. This is what sets biblical Christianity apart from all man-made religions. The best any man-made religion can do is to give us a *maybe* and then leave us hanging—waiting until death to find out what happens next. But the Bible says we can actually know our eternal destiny *before* we leave this earth:

> *Whoever believes in the Son of God has the*
> *testimony in himself. Whoever does not believe*
> *God has made him a liar, because he has not*
> *believed in the testimony that God has borne*
> *concerning his Son. And this is the testimony, that*
> *God gave us eternal life, and this life is in his Son.*
> *Whoever has the Son has life; whoever does not*
> *have the Son of God does not have life.*
>
> (1 John 5:10–13)

Our hope and prayer for you, dear reader, is that you have this same comforting assurance.

In a world filled with trouble and all kinds of suffering, what a comfort it is to have Jesus as our refuge, and heaven as our eternal resting place! Jesus gives the same gracious invitation to each of us: "Come to me, all who labor and are heavy laden, and I will give you rest. Take my yoke upon you, and learn from me, for I am gentle and lowly in heart, and you will find rest for your souls. For my yoke is easy, and my burden is light" (Matthew 11:28–30).

Life is hard, and our earthly tent is being torn down. We are not what we once were. "For in this tent we groan, longing to put on our heavenly dwelling" (2 Corinthians 5:2). Suffering is all around us, but if we are trusting in Jesus as Savior and Lord we have a sure promise. One day, our spirit will be delivered from our body of disease, disability, and death, and we will be clothed with an eternal tent that is imperishable: a building that is better than our current house. Therefore, "we are always of good courage. We know that while we are at home in the body we are away from the Lord, for we walk by faith, not by sight" (2 Corinthians 5:6–7).

# Study & Discussion Guide

### How to Use This Study & Discussion Guide

This guide is designed to be an aid to deeper understanding and application of biblical truths which are taught in this book. It is intended for individual and/or group study. For this reason, some questions will yield more profit from interacting with others in a small group. These particular questions have been set apart from the rest of each lesson under the heading "Let's Talk."

There are six lessons in this guide, corresponding to the six chapters in the book. The "Introduction" and "Conclusion" are grouped together with their closest chapter. Each lesson is composed of four basic parts:

○ *One-Paragraph Summary:* This is a quick reminder of the content and biblical themes presented in the corresponding chapter. This summary will be especially helpful if some time has lagged between reading the chapter and doing the personal Bible study, as well as being a simple way to introduce a group discussion.

○ *Key Thought:* This is a summary or restatement of the main point of the corresponding chapter in the book. Keep this in mind as you work on each lesson.

○ *Dig Deeper:* These questions are written to encourage you in further Bible study and personal reflection. If you are doing this study as a group, these questions should be completed prior to your group meeting. Your preparation will make your input more valuable to the group discussion.

○ *Let's Talk:* These questions are designed to stimulate group interaction in a shared learning experience. If you are doing this study by yourself, you may consider using them for further reflection as well.

## A Note to Discussion Group Leaders

If you are leading a small group through the study of *When Disability Hits Home*, please keep the following guiding principles in mind:

○ BE SENSITIVE to the needs of your group and each participant's life situation. Has disability just entered their life or family? Are they still in shock over life-altering news? Is someone in their family currently hospitalized? Are they in the midst of a very difficult trial and simply need to be in a loving environment? Are they more of a listener than a talker? Ask the Lord to help you to be gracious and understanding.

○ CONSIDER including a light refreshment or snack. This is a simple way to create a more informal atmosphere, so that it feels more like a shared learning experience instead of a formal classroom. Seating in the round, instead of in rows, will make each person feel valuable to the group. Additionally, consider meeting in a home rather than a church building. This immediately lends itself to a more informal learning experience.

○ OPEN your discussion time with prayer. Thank God for the opportunity to learn together and ask for the Holy Spirit's help to understand and apply biblical truth. By the time the third lesson comes around, you should be able to discern who in the group might feel comfortable opening in prayer. If in doubt, ask the person privately before the meeting, rather than putting him or her on the spot.

○ READ the "One-Paragraph Summary" and the "Key Thought" and share how these have personally helped you gain further understanding and appreciation for God's wisdom and grace in your life. If you, the leader, display healthy transparency and willingness to share, you will quickly discover that others will let their guard down and open up.

○ GO AROUND the group answering questions from the "Dig Deeper" section. Some individuals may not be accustomed to sharing personal thoughts or experiences in a group setting. Be patient. Allow them to pass on answering a question, but as you progress further through the six-week study, gently encourage them to participate. Consider keeping a few Bibles on hand for those who are new to the Scriptures. If someone doesn't answer a question quite right, according to sound doctrine, gently offer correction or further clarification. Offer affirmation as much as possible along the way.

○ WALK YOUR GROUP through the "Let's Talk" section, encouraging each participant to share their thoughts.

○ CLOSE your discussion time with prayer. Be sure to ask if anyone has something they would like prayer for during the upcoming week. Again, once you have gauged the maturity and comfort level of your participants, consider asking someone else to close your time in prayer. Discreetly keep an eye on the clock, so that you are sure to allow time for prayer, but do not hinder group involvement by being a rigid clock-watcher.

○ **ALLOW TIME** for chitchat as people meander away from the group and head home. Thank each participant for being there and for their participation. For example, if a timid person took even a baby step in the right direction of group participation or life application, offer them a personal word of encouragement as they leave.

There are certainly other ways to grow as a discussion leader, but I offer these to you from the standpoint of what has worked well for me over the years. For further growth, I highly recommend the little book *Iron Sharpens Iron: Leading Bible-Oriented Small Groups That Thrive* by Orlando Saer.

## LESSON 1: Whose Fault Is It?
*(Introduction and Chapter 1)*

### One-Paragraph Summary

When suffering enters our lives we can be tempted to blame someone; that is, to make a direct connection between specific wrongdoing and specific consequences. Though the Bible does teach there are consequences to sin, and that all of life's griefs are the result of mankind's original sin, there is not always a direct cause-and-effect relationship between specific affliction and specific sin. Another temptation we face is to remake God into an image that is easier to accept or that we think fits better with our experience. Therefore, what is needed is a God-centered framework for how we think about God. This framework is built upon the foundation of God's sovereignty and providence.

### Key Thought

God's greater purpose in all things, including disability, is to make known the glory of his grace, which is made visible through the person and work of Jesus Christ.

### Dig Deeper

1. Read the first two chapters of the book of Job.
   a. How does God describe the man Job?
   *Your answer:*

b. Describe Satan's involvement in Job's suffering.
   *Your answer:*

c. What various kinds of suffering did Satan inflict upon Job?
   *Your answer:*

d. What do you see in the biblical text that points to God's authority over Satan?
   *Your answer:*

e. What was Job's response to his loss?
   *Your answer:*

f. When Job's distraught wife urged him to be angry at God, what was Job's response?

*Your answer:*

g. Even though Job later referred to his friends as miserable comforters (Job 16:2), due to their relentless attempts to blame him for his suffering and loss, their ministry of comfort to him during the first seven days was valuable (Job 2:11–13). Describe their ministry and explain why this is a pattern worth imitating in your ministry to others who are hurting.

*Your answer:*

2. Read Proverbs 3:5–6.

a. What do these verses teach you about yourself and about trusting God?

*Your answer:*

b. What is the opposite of trusting God?
*Your answer:*

c. What are three common ways you are tempted to trust in yourself or your own wisdom?
*Your answer:*

3. Read Exodus 4:11.
   a. What does God say about himself?
   *Your answer:*

   b. How does God's sovereignty in creation relate to his purposes for each person?
   *Your answer:*

c. What comfort and assurance do you gain from this truth?

*Your answer:*

_____

4. Memorize Romans 11:36.

## Let's Talk

After sharing your responses to the "Dig Deeper" questions, work through the following together.

1. Why do you think our default human response to suffering is to pin the blame on ourselves or someone else?

*Your answer:*

2. What do these default responses reveal about our view of God's character? In what ways might you be tempted to remake God in your image?
   *Your answer:*

3. Read and discuss Deuteronomy 29:29. What comfort and assurance do you gain from this truth?
   *Your answer:*

4. Read Psalm 135.
   a. Name the reasons the psalmist calls us to praise God.
   *Your answer:*

b. What attributes (characteristics) of God do you see revealed in this psalm?

*Your answer:*

c. What ultimately happens to those who make idols—that is, recreate God in their own image?

*Your answer:*

d. Respond to Psalm 135 by spending some time praising God together.

*Your answer:*

## LESSON 2: Where Is God in Our Suffering?
*(Chapter 2)*

### One-Paragraph Summary

Understanding the purpose of God in our suffering can be like trying to assemble a jigsaw puzzle without the picture on the box. But God always has a larger plan which we cannot see, a plan that involves more—but never less—than trials and blessings. The outworking of God's sovereignty on behalf of the good of his people is referred to as *providence*, which is put on display in both the trials and the triumphs of Joseph. Here we see the unfolding of a beautifully woven tapestry of sovereign grace, wisdom, and goodness. God was faithfully working behind the scenes, while innumerable and unexplainable trials were going on in Joseph's life, and, at every moment, God was compassionately attentive to Joseph's suffering. The same is true for you and me.

### Key Thought

Providence assures us that not only is God working out his master plan for the universe, but he is also at work carrying out his will for our good and his glory. This also means that God is not far away, but always present, near, and attentive to all of our ways and needs.

## Dig Deeper

1. Read Genesis 39–50. Write down every time you notice any indication that God was with Joseph.
   *Your answer:*

2. Read Ecclesiastes 3:1–11. How does Solomon's summary statement in verse 11 comfort you?
   *Your answer:*

3. Read Romans 8:18–39.
   a. How does the Holy Spirit help believers in Jesus Christ (vv. 26–27)?
   *Your answer:*

   b. What assurance do you find in verse 28?
   *Your answer:*

c. What good thing do you want God to do for you? How does verse 32 put that into perspective and encourage your faith?

*Your answer:*

d. When you feel like the whole world is against you, what truths from verses 33–39 help you put your confidence in the Lord? List them.

*Your answer:*

e. Why do the sufferings of this present life pale in comparison to the believer's eternal glory (verses 18–24)?

*Your answer:*

4. Memorize Isaiah 41:10.

## Let's Talk

After sharing your responses to the "Dig Deeper" questions, work through the following together.

1. Have you ever been tempted to believe that God has

forgotten or even abandoned you? Share your experience with your group.

*Your answer:*

2. How does the promise found in Isaiah 41:10 encourage you?

*Your answer:*

3. Read Psalm 16.
   a. What are the reasons for the psalmist's confidence in God?

   *Your answer:*

   b. How does the promise of God's presence bring assurance?

   *Your answer:*

4. Respond to the promises of God's presence by spending time giving thanks in prayer.

## Lesson 3: What Is God Doing through Disability?
*(Chapter 3)*

### One-Paragraph Summary

Physical disabilities provide a visible image of spiritual realities. In God's sight, we are all disabled. Every human being is blind, deaf, and cognitively disabled to some degree—in their heart. *Inability* is our greatest disability. It is what Jesus Christ came to cure. In the Gospel of John, we meet a man who was born blind. The disciples were more concerned with figuring out whose sin caused the disability. But Jesus surprises them when he says it wasn't the blind man's fault, nor the fault of his parents, but the man was blind by God's design—to bring God more glory. But the physical healing he receives is not the most important part of the story. Jesus didn't just open the man's physical eyes, he opened his spiritual eyes. The blind man got saved. Jesus healed his greatest disability: the blindness of his heart. This highlights the greater need which exists in every one of us, whether "abled" or "dis-abled": that our spiritual disabilities can be overcome only by the grace of God. This is why Jesus came to earth.

### Key Thought

Physical and intellectual disabilities remind us of the greater disability we all have been afflicted with through our genetic link to Adam. Apart from the gospel, we are spiritually disabled, but there is hope in Christ.

## Dig Deeper

1. Read John 5:1–17.

   a. List your observations about people and Jesus.

   *Your answer:*

   b. If multitudes needed physical healing, why do you think Jesus healed only one man?

   *Your answer:*

   c. Why do you think Jesus asked the man if he wanted to be healed (verse 6)?

   *Your answer:*

   d. What purposes of this healing do you see revealed in this passage?

   *Your answer:*

---

Read Luke 4:16–21.
   a. How did Jesus fulfill this prophecy in relation to our need as sinners?
      *Your answer:*

   b. Compare this spiritual description of our life without Christ to that found in Ephesians 4:17–19.
      *Your answer:*

   c. Read Romans 5:6–8. Describe God's rescue plan for sinners.
      *Your answer:*

   d. Memorize Romans 5:8.

## Let's Talk

After sharing your responses to the "Dig Deeper" questions, work through the following together.

---

1. Read and discuss Ephesians 2:1–10.
   a. How does the apostle describe our spiritual condition apart from Christ?
      *Your answer:*

b. What attributes of God went into action to provide for our salvation?

*Your answer:*

c. How is our eternal rescue achieved by the work of Christ?

*Your answer:*

d. What is the response God requires from each of us in order to be saved?

*Your answer:*

e. Good works come *after* conversion, not before. They are the fruit of salvation, not the root. Why is it essential to understand and maintain this distinction?

*Your answer:*

2. Read Hebrews 12:3–11.

Scripture teaches that Jesus endured the punishment that we deserve when he took our sins upon himself on the cross (for example: Isaiah 53:4–6; Romans 5:6–11; Colossians 1:18–20; Hebrews 2:14–15; 1 Peter 3:18; 1 John 1:9–2:2). Yet God disciplines those who belong to him.

   a. What is the difference between punishment and discipline? Talk through the chart *A Theology of Discipline* opposite, which is taken from the Shepherd Press book *Counseling One Another* by Paul Tautges.

   *Your answer:*

   b. Why is it important to understand these differences?

   *Your answer:*

3. Spend time thanking God for the full payment for sin that Jesus paid on our behalf, and also for the chastening love of God which trains us to walk in obedience. Consider singing the hymn "Jesus Paid it All."

## A Theology of Discipline

| | Punishment | Discipline |
|---|---|---|
| Nature | Punitive<br><br>*"I will punish the world for its evil, and the wicked for their iniquity."* (Isa. 13:11) | Corrective<br><br>*". . . but He disciplines us for our good . . ."*<br>(Heb. 12:10) |
| Motivation | Anger, wrath, hatred<br><br>*"Behold, the day of the Lord is coming, cruel, with fury and burning anger."*<br>(Isa. 13:9) | Love, responsibility, grief over sin<br><br>*"For those whom the Lord loves he disciplines, and he scourges every son whom he receives."* (Heb. 12:6) |
| Goal | To inflict penalty, to require payment for sin<br><br>*". . . dealing out retribution to those who do not know God and to those who do not obey the gospel of our Lord Jesus."*<br>(2 Thess. 1:8) | To correct, protect, and bless<br><br>*"My son, do not forget my teaching, but let your heart keep my commandments; for length of days and years of life and peace they will add to you."* (Prov. 3:1–2) |
| View | Dwells on the past<br><br>*". . . the Lord will repay him according to his deeds."*<br>(2 Tim. 4:14) | Hopes in the future<br><br>*". . . so that we may share His holiness."*<br>(Heb. 12:10) |
| Common response | Resentment leading to bitterness<br><br>*". . . men blasphemed God because of the plague . . ."*<br>(Rev. 16:21) | Sorrow leading to repentance<br><br>*"All discipline for the moment seems not to be joyful, but sorrowful . . ."* (Heb. 12:11a) |
| Result in the relationship | Abandonment/isolation<br><br>*"These will go away into eternal punishment . . ."*<br>(Matt. 25:46) | Reconciliation/restoration<br><br>*"But if you are without discipline, of which all have become partakers, then you are illegitimate children and not sons."* (Heb. 12:8) |
| End | Destruction<br><br>*"These will pay the penalty of eternal destruction, away from the presence of the Lord and from the glory of His power . . ."* (2 Thess. 1:9) | Change of character<br><br>*". . . yet to those who have been trained by it, afterwards it yields the peaceful fruit of righteousness."*<br>(Heb. 12:11b) |

## Lesson 4: Does God Make Mistakes in the Womb?

*(Chapter 4)*

### One-Paragraph Summary

It's no secret that society places a huge emphasis on being "normal." We tend to measure the value of others by whether or not they are physically appealing or "free from defect." But what if God looks at things differently? What if all human life is equally valuable—simply because every person is created in his image? Scripture portrays a mother's womb as God's art studio, the protected place where God accomplishes his creative purpose. Though we may wonder what the divine Artist is up to, especially when birth defects and disabilities occur in the womb, we can be confident that God's good and perfect will for each life is being carried out.

### Key Thought

In Psalm 139, the Holy Spirit provides a "biblical ultrasound," a picture of God at work, designing each and every divine image-bearer according to his purposes.

### Dig Deeper

1. What do the following Scriptures teach us about the Creator and creation?
   a. Genesis 1:26
   *Your answer:*

b. Exodus 20:6
   *Your answer:*

c. John 1:1–3
   *Your answer:*

d. Colossians 1:15–17
   *Your answer:*

e. Revelation 4:11
   *Your answer:*

2. How do the above Scriptures build your confidence in God as the perfect Creator who is worthy of trust and praise?
   *Your answer:*

3. Read 1 Samuel 16:7. What does this teach us about God's priority? How should this impact our view of a person with a disability?
   *Your answer:*

4. Memorize Psalm 139:14.

## Let's Talk

After sharing your responses to the "Dig Deeper" questions, work through the following together.

1. Read Psalm 8.
   a. What does this psalm reveal about God?
      *Your answer:*

b. What does it reveal about man?

*Your answer:*

c. Why is mankind the pinnacle of creation?

*Your answer:*

2. Read Jeremiah 1:4-5. What light does this Scripture shine upon the topic of God's presence and purposes in the womb?

*Your answer:*

3. Spend time praising God for being the wise and intentional Creator.

# Lesson 5: Dependent by Design, Disabled on Purpose
*(Chapter 5)*

## One-Paragraph Summary

God intentionally places the priceless treasure of the gospel in "jars of clay"—that is, in vessels of weakness. He does this to "show off" the surpassing greatness of the Savior. Additionally, God creates every person for his distinct purposes and, if we are willing, uses us with our impairments to confound the world's wisdom. The world may think people with disabilities are less important, but our God knows better. The apostle Paul accepted his "thorn in the flesh" as a gift from God because it kept him from exalting himself (2 Corinthians 12:9). In other words, it kept him humble. One of the hidden blessings of disability may very well be its promotion of an ever-present dependence on God, thus fighting the natural growth of our pride. Disability humbles us. It shows us how desperately we all need to lean on God's grace.

## Key Thought

In our weakness and suffering God's power is made more evident, not only to us who must rely upon it day by day, but also to those who observe us.

## Dig Deeper

1. What do the following Scriptures teach us about boasting?
   a. Jeremiah 9:23
      *Your answer:*

   b. Psalm 20:7
      *Answer*

   c. Psalm 34:2
      *Your answer:*

   d. Ephesians 2:8–10
      *Your answer:*

  e. 1 Corinthians 1:26–31
   *Your answer:*

  f. 2 Corinthians 10:13–18
   *Your answer:*

  g. Galatians 6:14
   *Your answer:*

2. What do the following Scriptures teach about pride and why God hates it?
  a. Psalm 138:6
   *Your answer:*

b. 1 Peter 5:6–7
*Your answer:*

c. James 4:1–6
*Your answer:*

3. How is humility of mind the solution to pride?
   a. James 4:7–10
   *Your answer:*

   b. Philippians 2:1–11
   *Your answer:*

4. Memorize 2 Corinthians 12:9.

## Let's Talk

After sharing your responses to the "Dig Deeper" questions, work through the following together.

1. Read and discuss 2 Corinthians 12:1–10.
   a. Review the benefits of weakness that are explained in this chapter.
   
   *Your answer:*

   b. Talk about Satan's role in Paul's suffering.
   
   *Your answer:*

   c. Discuss this statement: "That God rules over Satan without Himself being guilty of sin is a hard truth, but it is also comforting. It tells us that what we suffer from the Devil, his demons, and all evil is not purposeless but will lead to our good and God's glory."[22]
   
   *Your answer:*

d. How is it a comfort to know that God has Satan on a leash?

*Your answer:*

2. What does Paul's turning to God in prayer teach us about his perspective of disability and physical suffering?

*Your answer:*

3. Discuss how you see the biblical principles revealed in this passage of Scripture applying to your current life situation.

*Your answer:*

4. Spend time giving thanks to God for the ways you see his grace being perfected through weakness.

## LESSON 6: Doing Life Together in Gracious Community
*(Chapter 6 and Conclusion)*

### One-Paragraph Summary

The apostolic teaching concerning the church as a body opens a window to the brilliance of God's design. From our human vantage point, some parts of the body are weak or less important, and some are strong and appear more important. But each serves the purpose for which it was engineered by God. So it is in the body of Christ, the church. No single part is more important than another; every part is indispensable. In this way, disability draws attention to the value and necessity of every member of the body of Christ. In a world that glorifies human strengths and abilities, disability reminds us that the church cannot function without the weaker members. They truly are indispensable. Disability also blesses our churches by serving as a constant reminder of the temporal nature of our bodies. These bodies, which presently live under the curse of Adam, will one day be resurrected by the "Second Adam," Jesus Christ. Every believer will be glorified in his presence when Jesus returns. Scripture assures us: "Beloved, we are God's children now, and what we will be has not yet appeared; but we know that when he appears we shall be like him, because we shall see him as he is" (1 John 3:2). The human body is temporary, and so is suffering.

### Key Thought

God has designed his body, the church, to function so that it draws attention to the grace of the gospel. As a living body, the church should aim to function as such, with both strong and weak members living in full community.

## Dig Deeper

1. Read Ephesians 4:1-3 and answer the following questions.

   a. According to the apostle, we do not *create* a unity that does not exist, but are called to *maintain* the unity of the Spirit. How does this coincide with what you learned in Chapter 6 about the oneness of God's design in the church body?

   *Your answer:*

   b. What heart attitudes are necessary for this unity to be maintained?

   *Your answer:*

2. Read Colossians 3:1-17 and answer the following questions.

   a. What is already true of every believer in Christ (3:1-4)?

   *Your answer:*

b. How should these realities impact your spiritual vision and life pursuits (3:2)?
*Your answer:*

c. Since your old life is dead, and you are now alive in Christ, what kinds of life changes should you see (3:5-13)?
*Your answer:*

d. What heart attitudes and spiritual disciplines will cause you to grow in Christ and, consequently, be a greater blessing to your church family (3:14-17)?
*Your answer:*

3.  Read Romans 12:15–16. How can you begin to apply these biblical commands to how you relate to and serve the weaker members of your church family?

    *Your answer:*

4.  Memorize Romans 12:10.

## Let's Talk

After sharing your responses to the "Dig Deeper" questions, work through the following together.

1.  Read 1 Corinthians 12:12–26. Discuss the various ways we often fall prey to the two sides of self-focus, and how they negatively impact the church family.

    *Your answer:*

2. Read 1 Corinthians 13:1–13. Since the thirteenth chapter of 1 Corinthians follows the twelfth (originally, there were no chapter divisions), discuss how the supremacy of love should impact the way we care for one another in the church.

   *Your answer:*

3. Briefly discuss the encouragement found in 1 Thessalonians 4:9 and 2 Thessalonians 1:3. Informed by these verses, spend some time asking the Lord to teach you how to better love one another.

   *Your answer:*

4. Read Romans 8:28 and give thanks to God for his sovereignty, goodness, and wisdom in doing all things for his glory, which also turns out to be for our good.

# More Help and Encouragement

## LifeLine Mini-Books

Baker, Ernie. *Help! Disability Pressures Our Marriage.* Wapwallopen, PA: Shepherd Press, 2019.

De Courcy, Philip. *Help! I'm Anxious.* Wapwallopen, PA: Shepherd Press, 2018.

Deuel, Dave. *Help! My Friend Has a Disability.* Wapwallopen, PA: Shepherd Press, 2020.

———. *Help! My Grandchild Has a Disability.* Wapwallopen, PA: Shepherd Press, 2019.

———. *Help! My Sibling Has a Disability.* Wapwallopen, PA: Shepherd Press, 2020.

Deuel, Dave and Nancy. *Help! My Child Has a Disability.* Wapwallopen, PA: Shepherd Press, 2020.

James, Joel. *Help! I Can't Handle All These Trials.* Wapwallopen, PA: Shepherd Press, 2012.

# Books

Beates, Michael S. *Disability and the Gospel.* Wheaton, IL: Crossway, 2012.

Bridges, Jerry. *Trusting God.* Colorado Springs, CO: NavPress, 2017.

Kwasny, John. *Suffering in 3-D: Connecting the Church to Disease, Disability, and Disorder.* Wapwallopen, PA: Shepherd Press, 2019.

Lucas, Greg. *Wrestling with an Angel: A Story of Love, Disability, and the Lessons of Grace.* Hudson, OH: Cruciform Press, 2010.

Powlison, David. *God's Grace in Your Suffering.* Wheaton, IL: Crossway, 2018.

Tada, Joni Eareckson. *A Lifetime of Wisdom.* Grand Rapids, MI: Zondervan, 2009.

———. *A Place of Healing.* Colorado Springs, CO: David C. Cook, 2010.

———. *When Is It Right to Die? A Comforting and Surprising Look at Death and Dying.* Grand Rapids, MI: Zondervan, 2018.

Tautges, Paul. *Anxiety: Knowing God's Peace.* 31-Day Devotional. Phillipsburg, NJ: P&R, 2019.

———. *A Small Book for the Hurting Heart: Meditations on Loss, Grief, and Healing.* Greensboro, NC: New Growth Press, 2020.

# Blogs

www.counselingoneanother.com
www.theworksofGod.com

# Endnotes

1. D. A. Carson, *How Long, O Lord?* (Grand Rapids, MI: Baker Academic, 2006), 136.
2. Ibid., 46.
3. Nancy L. Eiesland, *The Disabled God* (Nashville: Abingdon Press, 1994), 69–70.
4. Ibid., 72.
5. Ibid., 83.
6. Ibid., 89.
7. Ibid., 90.
8. Ibid., 94.
9. Ibid., 100.
10. "Nancy Eiesland Is Dead at 44; Wrote of a Disabled God," *New York Times*, March 21, 2009, accessed November 30, 2017, https://www.nytimes.com/2009/03/22/us/22eiesland.html.
11. Ibid.
12. Theologians define providence in different ways, but here are three examples. Look for the common thread running through them:

    Wayne Grudem: "We may define God's providence as follows: God is continually involved with all created things in such a way that he (1) keeps them existing and maintaining the properties with which he created them; (2) cooperates with created things in every action, directing their distinctive properties to cause them to act as they do; and (3) directs them to fulfill his purposes."

    Henry Thiessen: "[Providence refers to] that continuous activity of God whereby he makes all the events of the physical, mental, and moral realms work out his purpose, and this purpose is nothing short of the original design of God in creation. To be sure, evil has entered the universe, but it is not allowed to thwart God's original, benevolent, wise, and holy purpose."

    Millard Erickson: "By providence we mean the continuing action of God by which he preserves in existence the creation which he has brought into being, and guides it to his intended purposes for it."

13. Randy Alcorn, *If God Is Good* (Colorado Springs, CO: Multnomah, 2009), 42.

14. Leon Morris, *The Epistle to the Romans* (Grand Rapids, MI: Eerdmans; Leicester: Inter-Varsity Press, 1988), 429.

15. This distinction between God as Judge and God as heavenly Father is explained more fully in my book *Brass Heavens: Reasons for Unanswered Prayer* (Hudson, OH: Cruciform Press, 2013).

16. William MacDonald, *Believer's Bible Commentary* (Nashville: Thomas Nelson, 1995), 1521.

17. Ibid.

18. Though not all are decisively biblical in their foundational understanding, three recent articles demonstrate the inherent danger that unborn children with disabilities face: "New Study: Abortion after Prenatal Diagnosis of Down Syndrome Reduces Down Syndrome Community by Thirty Percent," Charlotte Lozier Institute, April 21, 2015, accessed June 9, 2020, https://lozierinstitute.org/new-study-abortion-after-prenatal-diagnosis-of-down-syndrome-reduces-down-syndrome-community-by-thirty-percent/; Pasquale Toscano and Alexis Doyle, "Legal Abortion Isn't the Problem to Be Solved," *The Atlantic*, June 19, 2019, accessed June 9, 2020, https://amp.theatlantic.com/amp/article/592000/; Brian Clowes, PhD, "Shouldn't Abortion Be Allowed for Serious or Fatal Birth Defects?," Human Life International, May 22, 2017, accessed June 9, 2020, https://www.hli.org/resources/abortion-serious-fatal-birth-defects/.

19. Joni Eareckson Tada, *A Lifetime of Wisdom* (Grand Rapids, MI: Zondervan, 2009), 86.

20. John MacArthur, ed., *The MacArthur Study Bible* (Nashville: Word Bibles, 1997), 1769.

21. Anonymous; cited in Oswald Sanders, *Spiritual Leadership* (Chicago: Moody Press, 1967), 223–224.

22. "God's Devil," first published in *Tabletalk Magazine*, Ligonier Ministries, https://www.ligonier.org/learn/devotionals/gods-devil/.

 **joni&friends**

It is our great pleasure at Joni & Friends International Disability Center to endorse this book, *When Disability Hits Home*, produced by Shepherd Press. We pray this resource will bless you in your journey.

Joni & Friends is answering the call in the Gospel of Luke, chapter 14, "invite the poor, the crippled, the lame, the blind, and you will be blessed.... make them come in so my house will be full." Our mission at Joni & Friends is to communicate the gospel and equip Christ-honoring churches worldwide to evangelize and disciple people affected by disabilities.

We present the gospel of Jesus Christ to all people affected by disability and their families who are served through our programs around the world. We train, disciple, and mentor people affected by disability to exercise their gifts of leadership and service in their churches and communities. Visit us at https://www.joniandfriends.org/ministries/ to learn about all our ministries, such as Wheels for the World, Family Retreats, and radio and television ministries, and to find an area ministry office near you.

## CONTACT JONI & FRIENDS

○ Visit our website, www.joniandfriends.org.
○ For help and inspiration, visit:
https://www.joniandfriends.org/help-inspiration/
○ To find out how you can get involved, visit:
https://www.joniandfriends.org/support-us/

# Scripture Index

NOTE: this Scripture Index is not included in the e-book versions.

# About Shepherd Press Publications

- ○ They are gospel driven.
- ○ They are heart focused.
- ○ They are life changing.

## Our Invitation to You

We passionately believe that what we are publishing can be of benefit to you, your family, your friends, and your work colleagues. So we are inviting you to join our online mailing list so that we may reach out to you with news about our latest and forthcoming publications, and with special offers.

Visit:

**www.shepherdpress.com/newsletter**

and provide your name and email address.